Because, I Love You

Because, I Love You

Lynn Marie White

iUniverse, Inc.
Bloomington

Because, I Love You

iUniverse books may be ordered through booksellers or by contacting:

iUniverse
1663 Liberty Drive
Bloomington, IN 47403
www.iuniverse.com
1-800-Authors (1-800-288-4677)

ISBN: 978-1-4759-3127-3 (sc)
ISBN: 978-1-4759-3128-0 (ebk)

Printed in the United States of America

iUniverse rev. date: 06/20/2012

Contents

I praise You, Jesus, for choosing me to work with You. I am grateful to Your Holy Spirit for being my inspiration, for letting me hear Your voice and for guiding me.

During the course of writing this book, God reminded me several times of how He answers prayers. I want to give thanks to Mom, Dad and Mary for praying for my soul. They gave their time tirelessly for me to the Lord in prayer.

You never know how far God will take your prayers or where they will lead to.

I treasure my husband, Paul. I thank God for bringing someone so special into my life to stand by my side. The light, love, and wisdom of Jesus Christ shines through Paul and teaches me many things.

I am also grateful for Billie Jo's help despite her busy schedule.

I have used several different versions of the Bible because some were easier to understand or others painted a clearer picture.

KJV—King James Version

ASV—American Standard Version

LVB—Living Bible Version

RSV—Revised Standard Version

SIM—Simple English

NJB—New Jerusalem with Apocrypha

YGB—Young's Bible

WEY—Weymouth's New Testament

WEB—Webster's Bible

Lord, bless these words You have given me to share with others. I pray they speak to many hearts and bring blessing upon blessing to them. Open hearts, eyes and ears to receive what You have for them—in the name of Jesus I pray.

When you believe in Jesus Christ, He lives in you. He lives through you.

When you invite Jesus into your heart, you can now enjoy eternity with Him.

> *For God so loved the world that he gave his only Son, that whoever believes in him should not perish but have eternal life. John 3:16 RSV*
>
> *He that believeth and is baptized shall be saved; but he that believeth not shall be damned. Mark 16:16 KJV*
>
> *But he gave the right to become God's children to those who did accept him, to those who believe in his name. John 1:12 SIM*

If you'd only believe—

God spoke the words in bold print to me, and He told me to share them with you. He also spoke the Words in italics so you can embrace them.

This book is best when read slowly. Read a page or two; let God's words speak to you and minister to your heart. Let the Lord bless you. Then, pick up the book and read a little more.

I Want Us Together — God

I spoke for you before you were born. I spoke for you before the world began. I spoke for you again when I died on the cross. I called you.

Jesus prayed to our Heavenly Father about you specifically, the one He loves. He pleaded for your soul, your future, your safety, your life.

> *My plea is not for the world but for those you have given me because they belong to you. And all of them, since they are mine, belong to you; and you have given them back to me with everything else of yours, and so they are my glory! Now I am leaving the world, and leaving them behind, and coming to you. Holy Father, keep them in your own care—all those you have given me—so that they will be united just as we are, with none missing—I'm not asking you to take them out of the world, but to keep them safe from Satan's power. They are not part of this world any more than I am. Make them pure and holy through teaching them your words of truth.—I am not praying for these alone but also for the future believers who will come to me because of the testimony of these. John 17:9-11, 15-17, 24 LVB*

Jesus' heart is that you come to know Him and live with Him eternally. The very reason Jesus died was to save you from Hell. He died in hopes that you would accept Him as your Savior and live. Jesus has called you by name. Hear His voice. You are His. Receive His love.

> *But now the Lord who created you, O Israel, says, "Don't be afraid, for I have ransomed you; I have called you by name; you are mine."*
> *Isaiah 43:1 LVB*

I am calling to you. Come to Me.

> *But the Lord God called to the man, and said to him, "Where are you?" Genesis 3:9 RSV*

God calls to us. He knows exactly where we are, but He wants us to hear His voice, know He is near and know He is looking to us. Our Father loves us and calls us closer to Him daily. Our Creator craves fellowship with us.

I stand here knocking. Let Me in. Seek Me. I seek you. I am knocking. Let Me in. I desire a relationship with you.

> *Look! I have been standing at the door and I am constantly knocking. If anyone hears me calling him and opens the door, I will come in and fellowship with him and he with me. Revelation 3:20 LVB*

God not only knocks at the sinner's heart, but He daily knocks on the heart of the believer. Sometimes we get too busy doing our own thing in life, and we forget about our God. He waits patiently for us to answer the door and let Him in. Just like our best friend, He wants to come into our lives daily and communicate with us. God looks forward to the fellowship for which He designed us. The Bible tells us in 1 Chronicles 16:11 to seek the Lord, His strength and presence continually.

> *I don't want your sacrifices — I want your love; I don't want your offerings — I want you to know me. Hosea 6:6 LVB*

I long for you to sit with Me. I love you. I want you to be with Me. I desire a relationship with you. Know that I love you.

> *God called you into a relationship of sharing with his Son, our Lord Jesus Christ. God is faithful. 1 Corinthians 1:9 SIM*

When the Almighty Creator is telling you that He wants <u>you</u> to be with Him, don't you feel privileged? The author and finisher of your faith wants you to be with Him, in His presence. He desires your company. He created you for His pleasure because He wants a relationship with you right now. Don't just sit there—go for it! Get into God's word. Read your Bible; read the love letter He has written to you. Seek His face, and enter His presence by praying and worshipping the One who brought you life. He wants you to know, beyond a shadow of a doubt, how much He loves you.

It doesn't matter how close you are to Me, just as long as you are walking My way.

> *And Enoch walked with God, and he was not; for God took him. Genesis 5:24 KJV*

Enoch didn't start walking with God until he was 300 years old, but when he finally decided, he walked every single day with the Lord. Spending time with God brought Enoch so close to our Father that God just took him up to Heaven. The word Enoch means "dedicated." God gives us a choice daily to be with Him or not. Dedication to the Lord is *our* choice. Decide to walk with His majesty.

Do you have time for Me? You have time for religious things, but do you have time for Me? I desire your prayers and your time sitting at My feet.

Lynn Marie White

You may work for God as a Sunday school teacher, a preacher, a volunteer; you may feed the hungry and give to the needy, but are you paying attention to Him? Do you remember the One who has put you in that honorable position to do His work?

Have you said, "Good morning," to Him today, thanked Him for the little things in life, stopped to listen to His voice through the birds?

Or have you been too busy working *for* Him to *notice* Him?

Don't be like the Pharisees and Sadducees, putting actions and laws above God. Our Lord desires you to sit at His feet and just be with Him. You're His child.

> *Again I say, we are telling you about what we ourselves have actually seen and heard, so that you may share the fellowship and the joys we have with the Father and with Jesus Christ his Son. 1 John 1:3 LVB*

My words to you last forever. All this other stuff will pass, but spending time with Me brings you closer, brings you farther into My Kingdom. Don't you want to come closer?

Is My presence important to you?

Focus on Me—My love comes flooding over you when you focus on Me. If you succumb to the distractions, you are missing the opportunity to grow, to be closer, to draw nearer. You are missing the opportunity to be blessed. You will not know what you've missed until you are home with Me, but I want you to have all of My blessings right now.

In the course of their journey he came to a village, and a woman named Martha welcomed him into her house. She had a sister called Mary, who sat down at the Lord's feet and listened to him speaking. Now Martha, who was distracted with all the serving, came to him and said, "Lord, do you not care that my sister is leaving me to do the serving all by myself? Please tell her to help me." But the Lord answered, "Martha, Martha," he said, "you worry and fret about so many things, and yet few are needed, indeed only one. It is Mary who has chosen the better part, and it is not to be taken from her."
Luke 10:38-42 NJB

God tells us to seek *Him* first. He tells us that sitting at His feet is "the better part." Don't worry so much about everything; don't be distracted by menial tasks or even weighty troubles. Set your mind on the things of the Lord, and He will take care of them. It's true, chores do have to be done; life does goes on, but it should go on with Jesus on your mind. The enemy brings thoughts into your head and turns your thinking elsewhere. He doesn't want God's word penetrating our minds because it is LIFE.

Jesus is life. He is the way; He is health, peace and prosperity. He tells us to choose to sit at His feet, and we benefit by being in His presence. Business has to be taken care of, but the Lord wants us to live as close to Heaven as we can right now, here in *this* world. He loves to see His children happy and blessed.

And so, dear brothers, now we may walk right into the very Holy of Holies where God is, because of the blood of Jesus. Let us go right in, to God himself, with true hearts fully trusting him to receive us, because we have been sprinkled with Christ's blood to make us clean, and because our bodies have been washed with pure water.
Hebrews 10:19-22 LVB

It is through the love of Jesus Christ and His dying on the cross that we can now come to the Lord boldly and enter into His presence.

Good morning, My child, I have been waiting for you to acknowledge Me. I've been singing to you all morning. You were too busy in your own thoughts about the world to notice. I'm glad you finally heard My voice. Lots of birds sang for you today.

Don't you want to talk with Me? I love your presence. I am always with you, but sometimes you are not with Me. Your mind wanders, or you are interested in other things. These things are not important. My work is important; My love is important; My word is important. These things last forever.

Are you blessed or off doing something else, like your flesh wants to do sometimes? Isn't knowing I am right here with you, speaking to you, paying attention to you and knowing you are in My presence the most satisfying experience there is?

Not only do you benefit from being with Me, but you are blessed within and without. You get your questions and prayers answered. All that time you spent on other things could have been spent with Me. Aren't you glad you decided to be with Me instead? You did well in choosing Me.

> *Glory in his holy name; let the hearts of those who seek the Lord rejoice! Seek the Lord and his strength, seek his presence continually!*
> *1 Chronicles 16:10-11 RSV*

Our Father wants you to be with Him. He created you. He made you in His own image, to be like Him, to communicate with Him. God wants to be first and foremost in your mind and life. Our Lord desires to spend time with you right now because He loves you.

> *Seek the Lord while you can find him. Call upon him now while he is near. Isaiah 55:6 LVB*

We were created *by* Him and *for* Him. We were created to have fellowship with the Lord. In Genesis 3:8, it's clear that God walked with Adam and Eve in the Garden of Eden. He was with them. He intended for us to be in His presence all the time, forever. Our Father created us to have access to Him at every moment. Along came sin and separated us, but God gave us a way back to Him again because He wants us with Him.

God gave us Jesus who died for our sins, to show us how much we are loved. Because of Jesus, we can enter into our Father's presence now. We can go up to His throne, speak to Him any time we wish. We can be with Him eternally and share His love starting now if we ask Jesus to live in our hearts.

I desire to be with you. Desire to walk with Me as Adam did; desire to be with Me as Eve did. The rocks will cry out and worship Me if I so desire, but I created you to be with Me.

> *Thou art worthy, O Lord, to receive glory and honour and power: for thou hast created all things, and for thy pleasure they are and were created. Revelation 4:11 KJV*

I want us to be together. I do not like separation. I do not like divorce. Just as a married couple hurts when they divorce, I hurt. A mess, chaos comes from it. I want to be united with My bride. I came to earth to unite My people with Myself. I am love; I am not evil. My people have a choice to be with Me or stay with the evil one.

When my people turn from Me, My heart breaks. A piece of Me breaks off when they will not come back to Me or when they

sin. I rejoice when they repent. I have nothing to do with evil; it will not enter into My Kingdom. There is no separation in My Kingdom. There is unity, there is one body.

"Therefore, behold, I will allure her, and bring her into the wilderness, and speak tenderly to her. And there I will give her her vineyards, and make the Valley of Achor a door of hope. And there she shall answer as in the days of her youth, as at the time when she came out of the land of Egypt."

"And in that day," says the Lord, "you will call me, 'My husband,' and no longer will you call me, 'my Baal.' For I will remove the names of the Baals from her mouth, and they shall be mentioned by name no more. And I will make for you a covenant on that day with the beasts of the field, the birds of the air, and the creeping things of the ground; and I will abolish the bow, the sword, and war from the land; and I will make you lie down in safety. And I will betroth you to me for ever; I will betroth you to me in righteousness and in justice, in steadfast love, and in mercy. I will betroth you to me in faithfulness; and you shall know the Lord." Hosea 2:14-20 RSV

Our God invites us into His Kingdom by drawing us toward Him with His undying love. Even if we are rebellious, He still lures us into His peace and tranquility through His goodness and mercy. Jesus' life shows us everlasting life. We have the wedding invitation in our hands. The King of Kings has proposed to us. It is our choice to receive His amazing love or not. Our Father tells us to choose Him (Deuteronomy 30:19).

I have always loved you. You are My heart, and I am inviting you to live with Me forever. Our marriage is soon. The celebration will be soon, and it will never end!

My fruits are ripe; My table will never be empty. My river will never run dry. I will always fill you. I will always keep you

refreshed. You will lack nothing. My love will always flow for you; My love has always flowed for you.

> *Let us be glad and rejoice, and give honour to him: for the marriage of the Lamb is come, and his wife hath made herself ready. And to her was granted that she should be arrayed in fine linen, clean and white: for the fine linen is the righteousness of saints. And he saith unto me, Write, Blessed are they which are called unto the marriage supper of the Lamb. And he saith unto me, These are the true sayings of God.*
> *Revelation 19:7-9 KJV*

Our Father is calling out to us to give us the blessed gift of salvation and all the gifts that go along with it. He will pursue us until the last day.

You don't know how precious you are to Me. Your words cannot express how I feel about you. My love for you is indescribable.

> *You have ravished my heart, my lovely one, my bride; I am overcome by one glance of your eyes, by a single bead of your necklace. How sweet is your love, my darling, my bride. How much better it is than mere wine. The perfume of your love is more fragrant than all the richest spices. Your lips, my dear, are made of honey. Yes, honey and cream are under your tongue, and the scent of your garments is like the scent of the mountains and cedars of Lebanon. My darling bride is like a private garden, a spring that no one else can have, a fountain of my own. You are like a lovely orchard bearing precious fruit, with the rarest of perfumes; nard and saffron, calamus and cinnamon, and perfume from every other incense tree, as well as myrrh and aloes, and every other lovely spice. You are a garden fountain, a well of living water, refreshing as the streams from the Lebanon mountains. Song of Solomon 4:9-15 LVB*

Nobody can comprehend the depths of the Lord's love; it is beyond words. This verse provides just a glimpse of how He feels about us, His bride. Jesus loves us so much He gave up His life so we could live with Him. The vastness of our Creator's love dwarfs the heavens.

> *For thy lovingkindness is great above the heavens; And thy truth reacheth unto the skies. Psalm 108:4 ASV*

My Love Is For You — God

I want to give My love to you. I have so much love, it overflows. I want to share with you. I want to share with all My people. You can have your heart's desires when you receive My love. My love is bursting like the sunshine. I love not only believers; I love all. My love reaches to the ends of the earth. My love plumbs the depths of the sea and exceeds the highest star above. I have enough for those who believe in Me and for those who don't believe.

I have enough love for those who sin over and over again. My love covers all. I am a forgiving God. I am the Creator. I know all your flaws. I created you that you could turn again to Me. I give you a choice; choose Me. I will give My love to you unconditionally. Seek Me; ask Me into your heart.

Ask Me again. You can never receive too much of Me. I hear your prayers. I hear your cries. Make My word the center of your life. Jesus is My word. Jesus is My Love. My love is for you.

> *For God so loved the world, that he gave his only begotten Son, that whosoever believeth in him should not perish, but have everlasting life.*
> *John 3:16 KJV*

God is pure love; all that He has for you is love and goodness. All that He wants to give you is love. Our Creator loves you just the way you are. He knew you would be rebellious. He knew you would sin; He knew you would turn away, but He also knows when you will turn back. This is why He sent His Son to die, so you could turn back to Him, so you could come back into His open arms. When you accept Jesus, you're accepting His word as truth. He gives you a choice to be with Him. He even tells you which choice to pick.

> *I call heaven and earth to record this day against you, that I have set before you life and death, blessing and cursing: therefore choose life, that both thou and thy seed may live: Deuteronomy 30:19 KJV*

Our Father wants you to choose to live in His love. He has so much to give. More than you can ever imagine.

I love you, My child. I tell you this to remind you. I show you *daily*. I shower you with gifts *daily*. My presents are all around you. I tell you, "I love you," because you need to be reminded. You are to show others My love so they can see My presents, My *presence*.

Jesus is My love. Some people don't know love; they have never seen it. They do not recognize true love. Some of My children think love is to be bought. Some think it is cruel; others think it is painful. My love is not any of those things. It is true and pure. My love flows; it does not hurt; it is gentle; it is kind; it is from Me.

> *Love is patient and kind; love is not jealous or boastful; it is not arrogant or rude. Love does not insist on its own way; it is not irritable or resentful; it does not rejoice at wrong, but rejoices in the right. Love bears all things, believes all things, hopes all things, endures all things. 1 Corinthians 13:4-7 RSV*

God's love is amazing. We can't begin to grasp how much He loves us. He will forgive everything wrong we have done or even thought if we ask Him to. Our Father's love is free to all.

When we desire our Lord's presence, we can come to know Him and what He is about. We grow in His love, which molds us into His very image so we can show others. We realize that we are important in His eyes, and He wants us to let others know this, also. Some of His children don't know they are loved by the everlasting Father. We can share His love by telling them. God wants all of His children to come and sit in His mercy, to be with Him.

> *I love those who love me, and those who seek me diligently find me.*
> *Proverbs 8:17 RSV*

You think I can't love you. You think I can't wrap My arms around you, but I can. I am a big God. I can love you no matter what. I can forgive; I throw your sins as far as east is from the west. I no longer remember them. Lay them at the altar, and let Me love you. Receive My love.

> *He is merciful and tender toward those who don't deserve it; he is slow to get angry and full of kindness and love. He never bears a grudge, nor remains angry forever. He has not punished us as we deserve for all our sins, for his mercy toward those who fear and honor him is as great as the height of the heavens above the earth. He has removed our sins as far away from us as the east is from the west. He is like a father to us, tender and sympathetic to those who reverence him. Psalm 103:8-13 LVB*

A caring father on earth loves his child, no matter what. Wouldn't the Father who created us love us so much more? Forgiveness is why Jesus died and rose again.

Why wouldn't I love you, My child? I created you.

Are you not much more important than the grains of sand I have made that hold the earth together?

Are you not much more important than the mountains that show My majesty?

Are you not much more important than the stars that reflect My beauty?

I have given all of these things to you. I created you to love; I created you in My image. You are very special to Me. I designed you in love, and I desire that you love Me. The depths of My love go deeper than you know.

> *Long ago, even before he made the world, God chose us to be his very own, through what Christ would do for us; he decided then to make us holy in his eyes, without a single fault—we who stand before him covered with his love. his unchanging plan has always been to adopt us into his own family by sending Jesus Christ to die for us. And he did this because he wanted to! Ephesians 1:4-5 LVB*

Our Father created us out of His heart, to be loved and to love Him. We are His children. He shows His graciousness to us daily through His creations around us, if we would only open our eyes and see.

I keep reminding you so you'll know and to lift you up. I keep telling you I love you to fill you, fill you with goodness. To take away the doubt, to take away what the enemy has put in, to put back what the enemy has stolen. I tell you I love you to lift you higher, to encourage you, to show you I am the way. I am your Father in Heaven who cares for you. The entire world around you can tell you different, but know that I love you. I am reminding you over and over again. You can't hear "I love you" enough. I may be the only One who tells you. Hear My voice and know that it is true. Receive My love; let Me fill you with My goodness and joy.

Jesus prays this to our Father, about us, the ones He loves:

> *My prayer for all of them is that they will be of one heart and mind, just as you and I are, Father—that just as you are in me and I am in you, so they will be in us, and the world will believe you sent me. I have given them the glory you gave me—the glorious unity of being one, as we are—I in them and you in me, all being perfected into one so that the world will know you sent me and will understand that **you love them as much as you love me**. John 17:21-23 LVB*

Paul prayed for us, also. He prayed that we would know the love of God, how deep and wide it is, that God's love covers all.

His love covers <u>everything</u>.

> *And I pray that Christ will be more and more at home in your hearts, living within you as you trust in him. May your roots go down deep into the soil of God's marvelous love; and may you be able to feel and understand, as all God's children should, how long, how wide, how deep, and how high his love really is; and to experience this love for yourselves, though it is so great that you will never see the end of it or fully know or understand it. And so at last you will be filled up with God himself. Ephesians 3:17-18 (19) LVB*

God wants us to comprehend much. He really does love us, even though we will never fully understand how much or even know why. I think of how small and unimportant I am to this world, yet He loves me. He created the heavens, the mountains, all the stars, the winds, yet He thinks I am beautiful. He wants to remind you how important you are to Him.

You are the glimmer in His eye.

You are so loved by Him that He gave His only Son to die for you. Jesus died so we could live eternally with God. He wants us with Him.

> *Greater love has no man than this, that a man lay down his life for his friends. John 15:13 ASV*

My love continually runs for you. Just as a river constantly flows, My love is always flowing for you. Just receive it. My love is always around you, encircling you. Seek Me, and you will find it. When you can't see it, be assured, My love is still with you. My love is in you. I will never leave you. You don't know how important you are to Me. You are so valuable.

> *Hallelujah! Thank you, Lord! How good you are! Your love for us continues on forever. Psalm 106:1 LVB*

The love of the Alpha and Omega always was, always is and always will be continuous. God is love, and you are the object of His love.

> *Yes, Lord, let your constant love surround us, for our hopes are in you alone. Psalm 33:22 LVB*

God's love for you is immeasurable. He wants to be in your life, and He wants to use you for His glory. He desires His word to be in your heart. His river of love can flow through you when you hear and obey His voice.

Come Closer To Me — God

Come up to Me. I want to share what I have with you. My ways are much higher than yours. My thoughts are much higher than yours. I want to be the God of your day. I want to be the God of your sleep. I want to be the God of your job, your play, your everything. Come up to Me. I want to give you My riches, My blessings and all I have in store for you. They are much higher than your expectations. Come UP to Me.

> *For as the heavens are higher than the earth, so are my ways higher than your ways, and my thoughts than your thoughts.*
> *Isaiah 55:9 KJV*

The way you can come up to the Lord is through praise and worship, prayer, studying His word and just spending time with your Father. He loves to hear your voice in His ear. The Creator of all desires to be the God of your WHOLE life, not just part of it on Sunday. Come up to Him now. Reach out to Him; let Him lift you higher and higher. Don't wait until you're at rock bottom, and the only other place to look is up.

God wants you to have everything He has. He has good gifts. You are His child. He wants to share His blessings with you, and He delights in your happiness. Being in God's presence and His fellowship are total blessings in themselves, and He still wants to give you more! To bless is an act of adoration. God loves and adores you. You are the one to benefit from all His goodness by coming closer to Him.

Lynn Marie White

> *But earnestly desire the higher gifts. And I will show you a still more excellent way. 1 Corinthians 12:31 RSV*

You can live in the Garden of Eden. As you live in Christ, so you live in paradise. You are enclosed, taken care of, provided for and blessed by My waters. You have life abundant in My love. No one can enter in without My permission. No one can take away what I have given you. You can live in comfort, wanting for nothing. I engulf you in My love; therefore, nothing else is wanted. You can live in paradise with Me.

Accepting My love is all you need to do on your part. Look for Me, and you will find Me. My angels draw the sword up; you can enter in. You can eat from the Tree of Life. Jesus is that Tree. When you discover Jesus, you have discovered eternal life, divine love.

> *And he said, "Jesus, remember me when you come into your Kingdom." And he said to him, "Truly, I say to you, today you will be with me in Paradise." Luke 23:42-43 KJV*

The thief on the cross asked Jesus to remember him. In Hebrew, "to remember" means to stay, to abide, continue, dwell, to remain, to be present. This man asked Jesus to stay with him, to abide and dwell with him. He asked Jesus to be present in his heart. This is all it takes. As soon as we ask Him into our heart, He takes us in. We are with Him and will live in His Kingdom and goodness forever.

> *Let all who have ears give heed to what the Spirit is saying to the Churches. To him who overcomes I will give the privilege of eating the fruit of the Tree of Life, which is in the Paradise of God. Revelation 2:7 WEY*

When we are with the Lord—it's all we need.

When you are with Me, I give you your heart's desire. My love *is* your heart's desire. You and I are together. I own the cattle on a thousand hills. Since we are together, you have what I have. You have your heart's desire. You lack nothing. Jesus fulfills everything you want when you have My heart. Jesus is My heart.

> *The Lord is my Shepherd; I shall not want. He maketh me to lie down in green pastures: he leadeth me beside the still waters. He restoreth my soul: he leadeth me in the paths of righteousness for his name's sake. Yea, though I walk through the valley of the shadow of death, I will fear no evil: for thou art with me; thy rod and thy staff they comfort me. Thou preparest a table before me in the presence of mine enemies: Thou anointest my head with oil; my cup runneth over. Surely goodness and mercy shall follow me all the days of my life: and I will dwell in the house of the Lord for ever. Psalm 23:1-6 KJV*

Enter into My presence with praise; enter into My house with praise. My Spirit can move in praise. Open your heart.

> *Enter into his gates with thanksgiving, and into his courts with praise: be thankful unto him, and bless his name. Psalm 100:4 KJV*

Start entering into God's gates with thanksgiving, then go further into His presence with praise.

When I take you home, you will enter My gates with thanksgiving in your heart and praise on your lips. You can enter that gate, My presence, right now.

I love your praises; I inhabit them. Praising Me opens the doors of your heart so I can enter in and fill you. I love to dwell in your heart and be with you. Praise Me in the good times and in the hard times. Invite Me in. Know I am with you.

> *But thou art holy, O thou that inhabitest the praises of Israel.*
> *Psalm 22:3 KJV*

The word "praise" in this context means to be clear (of sound), to shine or make a show of, to boast, to be foolish for, to rave and to celebrate. We should let everyone know we are totally for God. "To inhabit" is to come in and sit down, to remain there, to abide and dwell. It also means to marry—we are His bride. God is there forever for those who praise Him.

> *By him therefore let us offer the sacrifice of praise to God continually, that is, the fruit of our lips giving thanks to his name. But to do good and to communicate forget not: for with such sacrifices God is well pleased. Hebrews 13:15-16 KJV*

I delight in your praises. I am thrilled with your worship. I am pleased that you draw near to Me. I want you to know I love you. Draw near to Me; I will draw near to you.

> *Draw near to God and he will draw near to you. Cleanse your hands, you sinners, and purify your hearts, you men of double mind.*
> *James 4:8 RSV*

The closer we come to God, the more He reveals Himself to us. As we talk with and listen to Him, our relationship with Him grows stronger. This is just like the way the conversations we have with our friends allow us to know them better. We know what is happening in their lives, how their families are, how they feel, what prayers they need. God wants to be our best friend. He wants us to know how He feels about us and every situation in our life. God wants us to know Him personally. What an honor to know the Creator wants to have a one-on-one relationship with us!

> *We have been given possession of an unshakeable kingdom. Let us therefore be grateful and use our gratitude to worship God in the way that pleases him, in reverence and fear. Hebrews 12:28 NJB*

God has given us an amazing Kingdom that we haven't even begun to comprehend. Through knowing the Lord, our eyes are opened wider to the wonderful blessings He has for us. Acknowledging the goodness of the Lord brings us closer to Him because we are realizing who God is and what He is about. Our Father desires love, praises, honor and glory from all of His children.

> *But the hour cometh, and now is, when the true worshippers shall worship the Father in spirit and in truth: for the Father seeketh such to worship him. God is a Spirit: and they that worship him must worship him in spirit and in truth. John 4:23-24 KJV*

Let My river flow; I want My river to flow. It will flow. Sometimes logs and sticks try to stop it, but praise Me. Continue to praise Me, and I will break through the dam. Then, My waters will flow all around.

> *Now when the priests came out of the holy place (for all the priests who were present had sanctified themselves, without regard to their divisions; and all the Levitical singers, Asaph, Heman, and Jeduthun, their sons and kinsmen, arrayed in fine linen, with cymbals, harps, and lyres, stood east of the altar with a hundred and twenty priests who were trumpeters; and it was the duty of the trumpeters and singers to make themselves heard in unison in praise and thanksgiving to the Lord), and when the song was raised, with trumpets and cymbals and other musical instruments, in praise to the Lord, "For he is good, for his steadfast love endures for ever," the house, the house of the Lord, was filled with a cloud, so that the priests could not stand to minister because of the cloud; for the glory of the Lord filled the house of God.*
> *2 Chronicles 5:11-13 RSV*

The priests had put aside their differences and chose not to look at the things that could distract them. They came together for one purpose—to praise the Lord and lift Him up. Any little thing could have stopped this unity. Because they chose to focus on praising God and nothing else, His Holy presence came in so strong that they couldn't even stand up anymore.

> *For I will pour water upon him that is thirsty, and floods upon the dry ground: I will pour my spirit upon thy seed, and my blessing upon thine offspring: And they shall spring up as among the grass, as willows by the water courses. Isaiah 44:3-4 KJV*

Our Lord *is* the living water (John 4:10-14). Without this water, we do not live. God pours His refreshing water over us. His love is constantly flowing to us. Sometimes we hinder the river of blessings when we're involved in our self too much and forget to bless others with the love He has given us.

Sometimes we get caught up in our own troubles and forget to praise Him for simply holding our hands and helping us through.

We forget to thank our Father for things He has done or for what He is going to do. The love of Christ abounds everywhere. It will never cease. Jesus' love flowed from the cross for us to forgive our sins, to heal us, to give us a life of abundance and life eternal with Him. We have to remember to praise our Lord in everything and let Him break through the dam that tries to stop the flow. Let His presence overtake you, and pass it on to others.

I am here. Can't you feel My presence? I am walking right here with you. The living waters are here. I am the living waters. Step in; immerse yourself. Your praises are a sweet fragrance to Me. Your praises have entered into My gates. You are so precious to Me. Slip into My presence. I am in this building with you. Rejoice! I am here! Enter in. Enter into My presence.

> *I will sing unto the Lord as long as I live: I will sing praise to my God while I have my being. My meditation of him shall be sweet: I will be glad in the Lord. Psalm 104:33-34 KJV*

You can enter into My Holy of Holies daily. You can go in anytime you want. Coming into My presence requires you to surrender. Surrender your will; submit to My will. Surrender yourself. Every time you enter in, you can go deeper and deeper into My presence. You can see more and more of Me; I reveal more of Myself, My love. Each time you are in My presence, you lose part of yourself because the love of self cannot enter into My presence.

When you go back into the world, do not put your old self back on. Stay in the clothing I have given you. Stay in My righteousness. Stay in My love.

> *For Jehovah is righteous; he loveth righteousness: The upright shall behold his face. Psalm 11:7 ASV*

We are to give up our own desires daily, stay in God's righteousness and submit to His will. We can live in His presence.

> *For those who live according to the flesh set their minds on the things*
> *of the flesh, but those who live according to the Spirit set their minds*
> *on the things of the Spirit. To set the mind on the flesh is death, but*
> *to set the mind on the Spirit is life and peace. For the mind that is set*
> *on the flesh is hostile to God; it does not submit to God's law, indeed*
> *it cannot; and those who are in the flesh cannot please God. But you*
> *are not in the flesh, you are in the Spirit, if in fact the Spirit of God*
> *dwells in you. Any one who does not have the Spirit of Christ does*
> *not belong to him. But if Christ is in you, although your bodies are*
> *dead because of sin, your spirits are alive because of righteousness.*
> *Romans 8:5-10 RSV*

Our Father invites us into His house, His Holy of Holies. This is the Holiest place there is anywhere in the universe. This is the furthest place from worldly cares. When we give up all our concerns and thoughts to focus on Him, we can enter into His love deeper and deeper. The Almighty tells us to seek Him, look for Him, forget about everything else and become immersed in His goodness.

With all thanks to Jesus Christ, we can enter in. We are to leave our cares at the door, never to pick them up again, and then keep all the blessings our Father has handed us when we return to our daily routines. Every time we step closer to God, we receive more of what He has for us: more wisdom, more knowledge, more comfort, peace, joy and goodness. These eternal treasures become very important to us. The temporary troubles we have here on this earth become smaller when we realize our Daddy can take care of them better than we can.

Children have no worries such as these. You must become like a child, trusting and willing and believing in Me. A little child

shares everything he has without even thinking about it. Come as a child; share everything; give everything to Me.

> *I am telling you the truth: You must accept God's kingdom as a little child accepts things, or you will never enter it! Mark 10:15 SIM*

Give all you have to the Lord. Give Him your troubles; give Him your heart; give Him your life. Trust Him with all, just as a child trusts, believes and gives. Accept all that the Lord has.

Your whole life changes when you lay everything down and walk into His presence. Jehovah invites you in because He loves you and wants you to grow in His ways.

I love your presence, too, My child. I love when you call on Me. Just as you want to be wanted and needed, so do I. I am pleased to be wanted by you. I am delighted to be needed by you. I am overjoyed, and it delights Me when you call on Me for anything. I like to have your attention. This way I can show you My love. My love grows in you through our closeness.

When you call on Me, others around know. They see Me; they witness My glory. Make sure you keep reaching out for Me, for whatever you need or want. I am pleased you ask Me for it. I am the supplier. Your faith in Me is My delight. I am the One who blesses. I am the One who makes things possible.

> *Finally, brothers, we gave you instructions about how you must live to please God. You are living that way now. We are asking; yes begging, you in the Lord Jesus to do even more! 1 Thessalonians 4:1 SIM*

The Lord is asking us to please Him, and it is our faith that pleases God. Seeking the Lord and His ways also gives Him pleasure.

> *But without faith it is impossible to please him: for he that cometh to God must believe that he is, and that he is a rewarder of them that diligently seek him . . . Hebrews 11:6 KJV*

Our love—the love we have for our Father—grows so much when we seek Him. He rewards us with blessings when we spend time with Him. Our Father desires us to be in His presence.

See You First Thing — God

I love to see your smiling face in the morning, and when you greet Me first thing in the morning, I am thrilled. Gladness overtakes me to know you are thinking of Me first. That is how it should be. Seek Me first in all things. Look to Me to lead and guide you with everything in your daily walk on this earth. I will bless you in every way when you are with Me. Nothing evil can touch you when you are by My side. No, the enemy cannot have you when you are in My hands. The enemy might try to fool you; he will lie to you; he will even try to deceive you. But, when you listen to My voice and know that I am here, you will be comforted; you will know the truth.

> *When a man's ways please the Lord, he maketh even his enemies to be at peace with him. Proverbs 16:7 KJV*

Our Father tells us to seek Him first, before everything. This is for a reason. It is to prepare us for the day ahead. We are to be covered in prayer, our family covered in prayer. When God is first in our mind and heart, the enemy does not have room to come in. The Lord protects us from all evil. The devil may try to throw his evil plans at us, but our Protector has us in the palm of His hand. We can know that the adversary is taken care of when we look to our Father first.

There are times when you don't feel as close to your spouse or children, yet they are in your heart always. There are times for closeness and times for separation. These changing seasons are an integral part of your work here on earth. There is a time for rest, a time for work, a time for replenishment and refreshing. You need all of these times to revolve. You cannot have one without the other. This is My plan.

I know when you are busy, when you need rest and also the time you need to be refreshed. It is not always feasible for you to be basking in My presence. It is nice but not always necessary. Remember one of the lepers I cured? He wanted to stay with Me, but I had work for him to do. It was time for him to tell of My love.

Mary of Bethany chose to sit at My feet, but she needed it. She chose to be with Me, and I allowed it. She needed to be refreshed at that time. Martha, her sister, was doing work that had to be done, but she had the wrong attitude. Her working was not less important than sitting in My presence, but she could still seek Me. She could still pay attention to what I was teaching if her mind was on Me at all times. I would reveal to her what she needed to hear.

So don't fret while you are doing work for Me, no matter how miniscule. I am still with you; I will still speak. If you will listen, you can hear and still be close to Me.

FOR EVERYTHING there is a season, and a time for every matter under heaven: a time to be born, and a time to die; a time to plant, and a time to pluck up what is planted; a time to kill, and a time to heal; a time to break down, and a time to build up; a time to weep, and a time to laugh; a time to mourn, and a time to dance; a time to cast away stones, and a time to gather stones together; a time to embrace, and a time to refrain from embracing; a time to seek, and a time to lose; a time to keep, and a time to cast away; a time to rend, and a time to sew; a time to keep silence, and a time to speak; a time to love, and a time to hate; a time for war, and a time for peace.
Ecclesiastes 3:1-8 RSV

There is an order for everything—in the beginning, I made the heavens and the earth. When you put first things first, everything else falls into place. The earth was void, without shape. It was a chaotic mass. Without the heavens being first, where would the earth be? Could it stand alone? And without the earth being dark, what good would My light do? The earth would not benefit from the light. Eyes would not need to be opened clearly. If the light was already there, separation from light and dark would not happen. Everything has an order; stay in that order. Stay in My will. Seek the Kingdom of the Lord first—and all things will work for My glory.

> *In the beginning God created the heaven and the earth. And the earth was without form, and void; and darkness was upon the face of the deep. And the Spirit of God moved upon the face of the waters. And God said, Let there be light: and there was light. And God saw the light, that it was good: and God divided the light from the darkness. And God called the light Day, and the darkness he called Night. And the evening and the morning were the first day. And God said, Let there be a firmament in the midst of the waters, and let it divide the waters from the waters. Genesis 1:1-6 KJV*

God put everything in order, first things first. We are to follow that order. We should put Him first, the heavenly things first—His Kingdom first. Our self comes second. We are representative of the earth as we are made from the earth. God has devised a plan for us, so when we follow it, we are in His will and in His order.

When you seek Me in the morning, before anything, you receive special gifts. No one else can have these special gifts if they do not put Me first. They cannot see the gifts I had originally set aside for them.

I give you the sunrise. It only comes in the morning, before all else. When you put Me first, you receive more blessings than you would if you seek Me later. You can hear what I have to say about the day to come. You can hear My words and gain wisdom and knowledge through them. After the situation is already underway or almost over, you can still call on Me, but you have missed out on what could have been an opportunity to see My glory beforehand. When you see My beauty and glory first, you can remember and hold on to it all day. If you forget, I bring it up to you again. I give you a special gift in the morning because you are a special gift to Me.

> *But seek first his kingdom and his righteousness, and all these things shall be yours as well. Matthew 6:33 RSV*

The Hebrew meaning of the word "morning" is "to plow, or to break forth." Before the seeds hit the ground, you have to plow. You have to break up the ground before anything can grow easily. If you break up the ground, and God is standing right there with you, the ground is holy. It is truly blessed. It will bring forth many blessings. The seeds will multiply and be fruitful, then multiply again. Your day will surely be blessed when you've broken through first thing, holding God's hand. Your day will be fruitful, full of God's blessings He handed you in the morning, in the plowing, the breaking through. We can look for our Father anytime of the day or night, but why not start each day with Him?

> *Plant the good seeds of righteousness and you will reap a crop of my love; plow the hard ground of your hearts, for now is the time to seek the Lord, that he may come and shower salvation upon you.*
> *Hosea 10:12 LVB*

Just as I give you rest each night so you can be refreshed in the morning, your soul and spirit need to be rejuvenated with My love. I give you a new day; I give you a new outlook. It is necessary to begin your day with Me so I can give you new blessings. It's like taking a shower in the morning; I clean you up and start you off fresh and new each day. The troubles of yesterday are gone; I will take care of the ones for this day. Keep your eyes on Me, and know I fix everything. Just stay in touch with Me throughout the day, and remember where your help comes from. Then in the night I give you rest, so you can be refreshed the next day to start over again. Sometimes you need extra energy and strength. I am that energy; I am that strength. Count on Me for these things. Lean on Me for the refreshing that I bring. If you call on Me, I am there.

> *The steadfast love of the Lord never ceases, his mercies never come to an end; they are new every morning; great is thy faithfulness.*
> *Lamentations 3:22-23 RSV*

Jesus is the refreshing strength that is needed each and every day. He is the One who keeps you going. He is your comfort and your rest. Looking to the Lord before anything nurtures you in His wisdom. Seeking after Him gives the renewing you need and helps you realize how much your Father really does love you.

> *The Lord is wonderfully good to those who wait for him, to those who seek for him. Lamentations 3:25 LVB*

God tells us to search after Him so we can receive everything we need. He wants us to get closer and more intimate with Him. The Holy One is our supplier of peace and joy. It pleases Him to give us His heavenly gifts.

If you don't have Me in you, how can you know Me? My word is the reflection of Me, which has been written down for you to see. My Word (Jesus) has been laid out in front of you on the cross for you to see. How can you believe My word (Bible) if you don't know My Word (Jesus)? How do you know the truth if you

don't read My word? Study, seek, receive and know My love. You will be blessed.

> *Study to shew thyself approved unto God, a workman that needeth not to be ashamed, rightly dividing the word of truth.*
> *2 Timothy 2:15 KJV*

Keep in God's Word so you can know who He is, how He acts, what He does. You can come to know the heart of the Lord by studying the word He gave us. You will hear His voice, and you will be blessed.

Can You Hear Me Now? — God

❧

> *My sheep hear my voice, and I know them, and they follow me: And I give unto them eternal life; and they shall never perish, neither shall any man pluck them out of my hand. John 10:27-28 KJV*

Not everyone sees as you see, My child. Your eyes are opening to the many wonderful things I have in store for you. Keep delving deeper and deeper. Continue to search for Me. Keep looking My way. I will teach you and guide you the way I want to. I will teach you My ways. I will be your guide. Your eyes have seen nothing compared to what I have in store for you. I have more than you can fathom in your imagination.

Keep your heart and ears open. You will hear more from Me. I desire our conversations. I look forward to them. I desire communication with you. You are My child, and I love you; stay close to Me. I have much to share with you. Just as a father desires to give to his children, I desire to give to you. You hear My voice and grow stronger and wiser each day. I offer you knowledge and wisdom, and you hear. Listen and obey when I ask of you. Your reward will be great. I offer you peace and tranquility in your life. I give you love, and I give you kisses. I look forward to spending time with you. I'm even gladly anticipating spending eternity with you.

> *But blessed are your eyes, for they see: and your ears, for they hear.*
> *For verily I say unto you, That many prophets and righteous men*
> *have desired to see those things which ye see, and have not seen them;*
> *and to hear those things which ye hear, and have not heard them.*
> *Matthew 13:16-17 KJV*

A child of God is truly blessed at hearing his Father's voice.

You cannot ask questions without waiting for an answer. You cannot do all the talking and expect to have a conversation. Remember, I really am right here with you, not so afar in the heavens that I cannot hear. Even if you don't let Me in, I am still next to you. Listen for My voice through anything and everything I have created for you. I do answer your questions; I do hear your voice. Listen for Mine. I desire two-way conversations. When you hear My voice, it blesses you, for My word is the blessing.

> *And the Lord came, and stood, and called as at other times, Samuel,*
> *Samuel. Then Samuel answered, Speak; for thy servant heareth.*
> *1 Samuel 3:10 KJV*

The name Samuel comes from the root words "shama," which means "to hear intelligently" (often with attention and obedience), and "el," which means mighty, strength, as in the Almighty. Samuel heard our Almighty Father. God comes to talk to us; He wants us to listen for His voice. The Lord wants us to hear what He has to say. We can't come into His presence, talk to Him and ask for everything that we want, and then turn around and leave. This is not considered a two-way conversation. We should be like Samuel and say, "Speak, Lord, for Your servant is listening."

When you are praying is when you can hear Me most. When you are seeking Me is when you are paying attention to Me and can hear My voice. If you are looking to Me for the answer, you

will listen. **If you are not looking to Me for the answer, you are not going to hear very well.** Just as when somebody is talking to you, but you have other things on your mind, you will not hear very well.

If you sit and be still, you will hear. The more you seek Me, the more you will recognize My voice. I call you every day. I want to talk with you every day. Just as I walked and talked with Adam and Eve, I want to walk with you on a daily basis. I don't only want you to be with Me once or even twice a day, I want to talk with you constantly. You can learn more and receive more while you walk with Me. I am always here, but sometimes you forget about Me. I don't want to be on the sidelines. I want to be in the middle of your life. I don't want to be left out of your life; I want to be the center of it. I want to be in your heart.

Listen closely, I will speak. I will tell you things to come. I will tell you which way to go. I will tell you when to go. I will speak peace to you and tell you I am in control. I will speak and give you strength. I will speak—oh, if only you are willing to listen. Praying and listening keeps you close to Me. It teaches you to look My way. When you are done with your petitions, wait for My comforting voice. I will answer. Sit still and wait. Pray without ceasing, but be sure and listen for My voice. Seek Me all day long. I am with you all day and all night. You <u>can</u> hear Me when I speak.

> *His conversation is sweetness itself, he is altogether lovable. Such is my love; such is my friend, O daughters of Jerusalem.*
> *Song of Solomon 5:16 NJA*

God's Words are the most desirable thing in the earth. They are sweetness itself. His voice is preciousness. We can have all the goodness we want if we are willing to hear. He is our friend and loves us completely. Hearing God's voice allows His love to fill us.

You hear My voice in the morning more clearly because you are focused on Me. The day is new. You want to be with Me, you have been before and you know I am with you. The world around you has not yet begun to influence and come into your mind yet. Your heart is set on Me; therefore, your spirit hears My Spirit. My Holy Spirit is speaking, and you are listening. This is why it is so important to set your time aside to be with Me and Me alone. You can hear so much, learn so much and grow in My ways each and every day. Sometimes there are extreme circumstances where our intimate time together is not possible, but I know the situation. I am still with you. We are still together. Know that you can still hear My voice if you listen.

> *Cause me to hear thy lovingkindness in the morning; for in thee do I trust: cause me to know the way wherein I should walk; for I lift up my soul unto thee. Psalm 143:8 KJV*

Our Lord wants to be included in our daily routines from the beginning. Our entire schedule is of interest to Him. When we hear our Father speak first thing in our day, we are hearing His truth, and our faith is being built up. We can hear God's voice more clearly when we are focused on Him, and we stop to listen.

Listening to My voice is very important, and heeding My Holy Spirit is vital to your life. I bring blessing and life through My Spirit. When you don't obey My voice, death and destruction can result.

Listen more intently for My voice, because My Spirit is calling. Listen carefully, and you will know My voice. My Holy Spirit *is* My voice. When in doubt, wait for an answer. If there is confusion, it is not Me. Wait upon the Lord, be patient to learn what I have to say. Your situation or circumstance can pass by without you hearing My voice, but that is because you did not ask Me, or you did not listen for Me.

I will guide you daily if you stop talking every once in a while and listen. My voice is so very important to you, to your life and those around you. I love you, My child, and I want you to have Me and all I have to offer you.

> *And your ears shall hear a word behind you, saying, "This is the way, walk in it," when you turn to the right or when you turn to the left.*
> *Isaiah 30:21 RSV*

Our Father guides us every day, every step of the way. We have the opportunity to hear Him and know the ways of righteousness because His Spirit is in our spirit.

> *But he who is united to the Lord becomes one spirit with him.*
> *1 Corinthians 6:17 RSV*

You hear My voice through your heart. We mingle together because I am in you. My will is becoming your will. Sometimes you think you're in the way or your thoughts get in the way, but I will tell you if I am speaking or you are thinking. Don't despair, as you *will* know the truth.

I am the truth. I am the light. My light comes shining through. You will know if your thoughts are right or wrong. Your thoughts are not necessarily wrong all the time, but My ways and words are *always* the right way. My word touches you because I am the word. My spoken word is My love; it is Me. When My word is spoken and you receive it, you receive Me and My love; therefore, your whole being is touched. It is a free gift to you. I am freely given. Any and all may receive. It is My will that all receive My love. Jesus is My love. My word is My love. Love is who I am.

> *. . . Son of man, all my words that I shall speak to you receive in your heart, and hear with your ears. Ezekiel 3:10 RSV*

There's nothing between us. I am in your heart, and you are in Mine!

> *For by one Spirit we were all baptized into one body —Jews or Greeks, slaves or free —and all were made to drink of one Spirit.*
> *1 Corinthians 12:13 RSV*

Being God's children, we have His Spirit within us, and His Spirit helps us understand His voice with more clarity. Our Heavenly Father continually teaches us, speaks to us, gives us His love. Each deposited word is a revelation of the Lord Himself. When we hear and accept this word, we are allowing His love and goodness to penetrate us. We grow in wisdom and knowledge with each tidbit we receive.

> *And he said, Unto you it is given to know the mysteries of the kingdom of God: but to others in parables; that seeing they might not see, and hearing they might not understand. Luke 8:10 KJV*

Sometimes people act on their feelings. They believe they have heard My voice. Individuals often express their own feelings toward others, thinking it is from Me. But My voice is gentle, not hurtful. My word only causes discomfort to those in sin. My voice is wisdom and knowledge, not opinion. My voice is comfort, not pain. My voice is freedom, not bondage; conviction, not condemnation. I lift up; I do not put down. People can be hurtful when they speak, but seek Me, I will comfort. Ask Me if their words are of Me, and I will let you know. I am the truth.

> *But everyone who prophesies to people is speaking to build them up, to encourage them, and to comfort them. 1 Corinthians 14:3 SIM*

The word "opinion" means "divided, disbranched." Many well-intentioned people voice their own *opinions* of what they believe God has said. Unfortunately, many of these opinions are "divided" from the word of God. It's so important to make sure what was supposedly said by God can be supported in the Bible. Ask God; He will show you. God's word doesn't hurt or tear down; He builds up. The enemy will attempt to tear us down by lying in our ears, but God's Holy Spirit is our teacher.

> *I write this to you about those who would deceive you; but the anointing which you received from him abides in you, and you have no need that any one should teach you; as his anointing teaches you about everything, and is true, and is no lie, just as it has taught you, abide in him. 1 John 2:26-27 RSV*

Consult Me in all decisions, and I will answer. Wait for My answer. Don't strain to hear; just listen. You recognize My voice. Keep walking with Me. I will guide you and let you know, beyond a shadow of a doubt, that it's Me talking.

> *Ask, and it will be given you; seek, and you will find; knock, and it will be opened to you. For every one who asks receives, and he who seeks finds, and to him who knocks it will be opened.*
> *Matthew 7:7-8 KJV*

All we have to do is ask Him and then listen for the answer.

I have waited for you to hear Me.

> *He who has ears to hear, let him hear. Matthew 11:15 RSV*

Every time we listen to God's voice we are being taught about His ways, His righteousness and His love. Hearing and obeying the Lord brings peace and contentment into our lives. Our Father wants us to hear His voice and has created us to follow His calling. When we choose to listen to Him, we choose His love.

> *His purpose in all of this is that they should seek after God, and perhaps feel their way toward him and find him — though he is not far from any one of us. Acts 17:27 LVB*

Everything I Have Is Yours — God

❧

I am the wind that blows. I am the One who brings life. I have many blessings for you. My waters make you grow. Receive My rain. Turn your face toward Me. I am your bread.

I will consume you with My fire. I will burn your unrighteousness, and I will cleanse you. Receive Me. Look toward Me. Keep searching deeper. You are in My heart.

> *And God said unto Moses, I AM THAT I AM: Exodus 3:14 KJV*

Our God is everything. He meets every need. He gives life and supplies all things. Our Lord refreshes us when we're thirsty. He feeds us when we're hungry. The common desire of humanity is to be loved. Jesus supplies that love.

> *And Jesus said unto them, I am the bread of life: he that cometh to me shall never hunger; and he that believeth on me shall never thirst.*
> *John 6:35 KJV*

Jesus never leaves you wanting. All you have to do is believe in Him. When you seek His goodness, He hands you His blessings. Our Lord cleanses you if you let Him. His word purifies when you receive Him in your heart.

> *I will bring the third that remain through the fire and make them*
> *pure, as gold and silver are refined and purified by fire. They will*
> *call upon my name and I will hear them; I will say, "These are my*
> *people," and they will say, "The Lord is our God."*
> *Zechariah 13:9 LVB*

Our Lord purifies, cleanses and makes us whole with His fire, which is His love and His word. His love washes sins away, satisfies the hungry and quenches the thirsty. His word causes life to grow like a flowering tree in the rain. Everything that the Lord has to offer is good, and He wants you to have all He has.

Take this cup which I give to you. Take what I am handing you—your freedom from sins, freedom from sickness, freedom from damnation, freedom from poverty. You are free to worship Me. All that I have is yours; it is good.

> *Now as they were eating, Jesus took bread, and blessed, and broke*
> *it, and gave it to the disciples and said, "Take, eat; this is my body."*
> *And he took a cup, and when he had given thanks he gave it to them,*
> *saying, "Drink of it, all of you; for this is my blood of the covenant,*
> *which is poured out for many for the forgiveness of sins."*
> *Matthew 26:26-28 RSV*

The whole reason our Savior died was to set us free. He redeemed us from the enemy. We are now property of the Kingdom of Heaven, and we are free from everything the enemy had planned for us. All we have to do is grasp this knowledge—take hold of it, receive it and digest it. Eating gives nourishment; drinking refreshes and replenishes. Jesus meets our spiritual needs in much the same way.

If you give Me your heart, I give you My heart, too. I do not withhold My love at any time. However, if I do not have your heart, My love will be received by the ones who will take it,

the ones who make room for Me. Just as there was no room at the inn for My Son to be born, sometimes there is no room in your heart. If you give it (your heart) to Me, I can fill it and form it the way I want to. I can shape it with My love. Give Me everything you have, and I will bless you in all you do.

> *And I will give you a new heart—I will give you new and right desires—and put a new spirit within you. I will take out your stony hearts of sin and give you new hearts of love. Ezekiel 36:26 LVB*

Our Father can do miracles with our lives if we let Him. He'll turn the hard heart soft, heal the wounded, fix the broken, mend the torn and fill the lonely. We only have to do our part first, that is surrender to Him. As we seek Him, our hearts and desires become more like His—filled with His love, joy, peace, light, forgiveness and all of His goodness. All of this is freely given by the One who loves us.

Just put forth your foot, and take the first step forward. When you take the first step, it shows Me you are willing to be with Me. It pleases Me. It is a sacrifice on your part. Seek Me. Sometimes it isn't easy, sometimes there are distractions, but you know that is only the deceiver trying to steal your blessings. Don't let him take them from you because he can't use them, anyway. He cannot receive My love; he is incapable. He cannot receive My peace; he does not know how to hold it. He cannot receive any of My blessings; he does not know what to do with them. They cannot stay with him because he has no basis on which to put them. He does not have the Rock to set them on. Make sure you look for My goodness each day, first thing, so you can have what I have for you.

> *The thief comes only to steal and kill and destroy; I came that they may have life, and have it abundantly. John 10:10 RSV*

Draw near to God, and He'll draw near to you. Walking with our Father keeps us blessed and out of the enemy's hands. Walking on our own leads us to trouble, sorrows and eventually death.

Just as you want your children to be happy, healthy and successful, I want you even more to be worry and stress free. I want you to accept My healings. I want you to accept My blessings. I want you to receive all that I have for you. I am love; you can have love. I am light; you can have light. My nature is good; you can have goodness. Follow after Me; stay in My will.

You are wonderfully made, and I created you. You are made in My image; therefore, follow after Me, and I will show you the way. You are entitled to all I have for you. I do not want you living in poverty; I do not want you sick; I don't even want you to be sad. I want you, above all, to be happy and healthy and prosperous, in your physical life, just as well as your spiritual life. Every time you accept Me in your heart, I bring you life more and more abundantly. I have abundant life to give. I have a giving nature. All that I have is yours. Just as you give to your child, I give to you.

> *Beloved, I wish above all things that thou mayest prosper and be in health, even as thy soul prospereth. 3 John 1:2 KJV*

Jehovah Jireh is our provider. He gives us what we need, and He wants to give us our heart's desires. Our Father provides our necessities and our abundance. He is the One who has given us every gift we have. Our provisions do not come from our job. Our happiness doesn't come from anything here on this earth; it comes from the love God has for us.

> *Every good gift and every perfect gift is from above, and cometh down from the Father of lights, with whom is no variableness, neither shadow of turning. Of his own will begat he us with the word of truth, that we should be a kind of firstfruits of his creatures.*
> *James 1:17-18 KJV*

We are God's children, joint heirs with Jesus Christ. We have legal rights to all God has. He wants to hand us blessing after blessing after blessing. Every time we believe more of His word, we receive more of His blessings. All we have to do is accept what He has for us.

> *For his Holy Spirit speaks to us deep in our hearts, and tells us that we really are God's children. And since we are his children, we will share his treasures —for all God gives to his Son Jesus is now ours too . . . Romans 8:16-17 LVB*

God's children can have everything that He has. The Holy One wishes to see us blessed.

I have the keys to eternity; I have the keys to all. Everything I have is yours. What belongs to Me belongs to you, My child. All I have within Me is yours; you are My heir. Take it. Take My love; take My mercy; take My peace into your heart and soul. There is no charge; it has been paid. I love you, My child. Understand that I love you with all My heart. I hold nothing from you. I do not keep anything from you that is good.

> *I will give you the keys of the kingdom of heaven, and whatever you bind on earth shall be bound in heaven, and whatever you loose on earth shall be loosed in heaven. Matthew 16:19 RSV*

"Key" in Hebrew is defined as "an opener." It comes from a root word meaning "to open wide, to loosen, to begin, to plough." It also means to break forth, to unstop and let go free. When you accept Jesus into your life, you begin to live in His freedom. You're handed the keys to His Kingdom, the keys to all of Heaven. They are yours, and they are free. You can open the door to the Holy of Holies, run into His presence and sit with your Father anytime you want to. You can take hold of anything that is in your Father's house anytime you want to. He shares His goodness.

These same keys can also remove the chains that bind people to the enemy. Sharing God's word can help them escape the hold the adversary has on them. Presenting the gospel opens the door of Heaven, which leads to the Lord's peace, mercy, forgiveness, love, truth, healing and all His goodness. God has given you the keys to His Kingdom; share the love they can bring and help others break through the restraints.

> *For in Christ there is all of God in a human body; so you have everything when you have Christ, and you are filled with God through your union with Christ. He is the highest Ruler, with authority over every other power. Colossians 2:9-10 LVB*

Through wisdom comes peace and security. My Holy Spirit is wisdom. You have My peace and serenity when you receive My wisdom. You come to know My ways. You know that I am God; I am in control. Through My wisdom you come to know that I am the caregiver; I have you in the palm of My hand. You realize that I am with you, therefore, it doesn't matter who is against you. I always take care of My children. Seek more wisdom; seek Me. I am all knowing; I am wisdom.

> *But the wisdom from above is first pure, then peaceable, gentle, open to reason, full of mercy and good fruits, without uncertainty or insincerity. James 3:17 RSV*

We can have this wisdom if we seek the Lord, if we listen to His voice. This is one of the gifts our Father would like us to have.

> *MY SON, if you receive my words and treasure up my commandments with you, making your ear attentive to wisdom and inclining your heart to understanding; yes, if you cry out for insight and raise your voice for understanding, if you seek it like silver and search for it as for hidden treasures; then you will understand the fear of the Lord and find the knowledge of God. For the Lord gives wisdom; from his mouth come knowledge and understanding; he stores up sound wisdom for the upright; he is a shield to those who walk in integrity, guarding the paths of justice and preserving the way of his saints. Then you will understand righteousness and justice and equity, every good path; for wisdom will come into your heart, and knowledge will be pleasant to your soul; discretion will watch over you; understanding will guard you; delivering you from the way of evil . . . Proverbs 2:1-12 RSV*

Listening to our Father's Holy Spirit gives us wisdom and peace in every situation and trial that we go through. We can have so much peace if we pray and ask Him *first*, then listen for His infinite wisdom.

Grace and peace are multiplied to you through My word. The more you know Me and My ways, the more knowledge you gain, and the more wisdom you obtain. You receive and know more peace; you can see more grace. Your eyes are open to My ways, and My ways are good. The further into My presence you come, the more you experience and learn from Me. You can obtain more of what I have. You come to understand the immense love I have for you. I have given you access to what I possess. You see more

of My mercy. My forgiveness is precious to you; My joy becomes complete in you. Your faith increases through My knowledge. You have no need for anything else because you understand that I am the supplier of all, and your life is complete in Me.

> *From: Simon Peter, a servant and missionary of Jesus Christ. To: all of you who have our kind of faith. The faith I speak of is the kind that Jesus Christ our God and Savior gives to us. How precious it is, and how just and good he is to give this same faith to each of us. Do you want more and more of God's kindness and peace? Then learn to know him better and better. For as you know him better, he will give you, through his great power, everything you need for living a truly good life: he even shares his own glory and his own goodness with us! And by that same mighty power he has given us all the other rich and wonderful blessings he promised; for instance, the promise to save us from the lust and rottenness all around us, and to give us his own character.*
> *2 Peter 1:1-4 LVB*

Have you ever tried to give a gift to someone
who didn't want to take it?

You probably took time to handpick it out for that person. You imagine the joy that will come to the receiver. When the gift is rejected—no matter how politely—your heart sinks.

How does our Father feel when
we don't take what He wants to give us?

My love is good. My love is simple, not complicated. I freely give it to everyone. Do you receive My love? Do you receive My presents? I am a sharing God. Love is sharing; love is giving. Some of My children think they are not worthy of love. They think they are not worthy of *Me*. I created them just the way they are. I made them, and I made you. You are worthy; that is

how I want you. **My love shapes you and molds you into being who you need to be for My Kingdom.**

Sit in My presence; stay by My side; feel My love; know My love; experience what I give you. I give you My Son. I give you My mercy, and I give you My all.

> *He who did not withhold even his own Son, but gave him up for all of us, will he not also with him freely give us all things?*
> *Romans 8:32 WEY*

He gave us Jesus, the perfect sacrifice that nobody else was able to pay. He gives us His gentleness, patience, kindness, rest, love and more. God wants us to recognize His characteristics and share them with others so they can know they are worthy.

I know all your needs before you do. I am the supplier. Would an employer not supply his worker's needs to get the job done? He also gives him a wage, a reward, a blessing for doing the job. I supply all you need to show My glory through you.

> *But my God shall supply all your need according to his riches in glory by Christ Jesus. Philippians 4:19 KJV*

When you are with Me, I give you your heart's desire. My love is your heart's desire. You and I are together. I own the cattle on a thousand hills. Since we are together, you have what I have. Jesus fulfills everything you want when you have My heart because Jesus *is* My heart.

> *The young lions suffer want and hunger; but those who seek the Lord lack no good thing. Psalm 34:10 RSV*

Just loving the Lord completes you.
Open your heart, and see what you have in Him.

I have given you many things that you're not even aware of. I have given you authority over the enemy. I have given you riches beyond what you can see. I have given you health and prosperity in My name. It is all for you. You are My child, therefore, it is yours.

I am a loving God, and I give to you. The more you listen, the more you become aware of what you have. The more you yield to Me, the more you are willing to receive.

I am a giving God. You have wisdom at your disposal; just listen. Listen to your heart; I am in your heart. You have knowledge; you can know My ways. My ways are *good* ways. If you'll walk with Me, I will teach you. I am your guide. You'll be able to see My beauty, My love, My encouragement. My Holy Spirit reveals these things to you.

> *Call unto me, and I will answer thee, and shew thee great and mighty things, which thou knowest not. Jeremiah 33:3 KJV*

Many gifts are given by your Heavenly Father, each one of them wonderful. All you have to do is ask and know that He will answer in His awesome way. Sometimes you don't even know what to ask for, but getting closer to the Lord and staying in His will reveals more of the blessings He wants you to have. God will also hand out special gifts that you haven't even prayed for just because He loves you. He knows your every need and want.

> *And whatsoever we ask, we receive of him, because we keep his commandments, and do those things that are pleasing in his sight. 1 John 3:22 KJV*

When God's commandments are kept, it pleases Him. He loves you. It's a delight to God when you walk with Him and stay by His side. The Lord has given you open access to everything He has, more than you even know, and it's right there at your disposal.

Drawing near to God turns your desires to His desires; therefore, you'll want what He has and not what the world has. This is why your Father can give what you ask.

> *Therefore I say unto you, All things whatsoever ye pray and ask for, believe that ye receive them, and ye shall have them. Mark 11:24 ASV*

You have asked, and you have received. Anything in My will, you have received. You ask in My will, and I do bless you with it. It's My desire to bless you. Keep walking with Me and receive all I have for you. I am glad you can see the windows of Heaven opening for you. I am pouring (blessings) out on you. Others around you will be able to see what I've done for you; it is for My glory that I bless you.

> *And this is the confidence that we have in him, that, if we ask any thing according to his will, he heareth us: And if we know that he hear us, whatsoever we ask, we know that we have the petitions that we desired of him. 1 John 5:14-15 KJV*

You Can Lean On Me — God

❦

I've invited you into the waters, into My living waters. Now I am asking you to believe more and more of Me. I am asking you to step out in faith. Totally rely on Me. I will hold your hand; I will hold you up. I will not lead you astray. I will not let go of you; I will not forsake you. Totally rely on Me for everything. Your faith is strong, and it is becoming stronger.

Keep seeking Me. Keep your eyes upon Me, and you will see even more miraculous results from your prayers. Your prayers for your lost loved ones are going forth. Keep your faith, and watch the unbelievers come forth. My people are getting stronger and stronger. The waters are for you to play in. Step out on the water in faith. Walk with Me; walk in faith. The more you step out in faith, the more strength you receive. The further you walk with Me, the stronger your faith grows.

> *And Peter answered him and said, Lord, if it be thou, bid me come unto thee on the water. And he said, Come. And when Peter was come down out of the ship, he walked on the water, to go to Jesus.*
> *Matthew 14:28 KJV*

When you fully trust in the Lord and put your faith in Him, nothing is impossible. All you have to do is believe and know that He is God. Without faith, it is impossible to please God (Hebrews 11:6).

> *And Stephen, full of faith and power, did great wonders and miracles among the people. Acts 6:8 ASV*

Keep going, My child. Things are going My way. Don't despair about things around you. Don't look at worldly things or listen to what the world says. Look My way. I am coming; I am on My way. Stay with Me, My child. I love you.

> *Behold, he whose soul is not upright in him shall fail, but the righteous shall live by his faith. Habakkuk 2:4 RSV*

Jesus is coming for us soon. No matter what the enemy tries to tell you, know that the Prince of Peace is in control. It's up to us to cling to Him and not look anywhere else. Our faith and trust should reside in His truth.

> *Finally, my brethren, be strong in the Lord, and in the power of his might. Ephesians 6:10 KJV*

My hand, alone, is on your shoulder. I have lifted burdens. Receive My yoke; it is easy. I have taken your troubles from you; receive My goodness. Don't look at the enemy, but look to Me. Keep focused on Me. Sometimes you grow weary, My child, but you shall not faint. I am restoring you. I am your keeper. Keep running. I supply all your needs, everything you need, everything you desire.

> *But happy is the man who has the God of Jacob as his helper, whose hope is in the Lord his God — the God who made both earth and heaven, the seas and everything in them. He is the God who keeps every promise, and gives justice to the poor and oppressed, and food to the hungry. He frees the prisoners, and opens the eyes of the blind; he lifts the burdens from those bent down beneath their loads. For the Lord loves good men. Psalm 146:5-8 LVB*

Jesus is the One who gives happiness, hope and joy. He is the One who frees the prisoners, opens blind eyes and keeps all promises written in His word. Our Lord and Savior lifts burdens from shoulders too weary to carry any more. You are completely provided for and protected in the Father's love.

In the midst of troubles and trials, I am your peace.

> *These things I have spoken unto you, that in me ye might have peace. In the world ye shall have tribulation: but be of good cheer; I have overcome the world. John 16:33 KJV*

You can always rely on God to help you through anything; His peace can flow over you if you look to Him and fully trust in Him.

> *And the peace of God, which passeth all understanding, shall keep your hearts and minds through Christ Jesus. Philippians 4:7 KJV*

I Made You Just For Me — God

〰️

I have made the sky blue; I have made the trees green. I like them that way. I have made the flowers beautiful colors because it pleases Me. I have created you the way you are because I like you that way. Everyone is different because everyone has a different job. I will use others in different ways. When someone listens, obeys and does My will My way, it is done right.

When you listen to Me and walk in My Spirit, you grow wiser. Walk with Me each moment. Everyone has a different walk, but My obedient children are walking on the same path in the right direction. I have made you the way you are to do the job I have for you; nobody but you can fill the position I have created for you. They are not the right size, color or shape. Nobody else has the personality or the thoughts that you have. You are the perfect person for the purpose I have for you here on this earth. Nobody can take your place; I like you just the way I made you. I love you and nothing can change that.

> *O Lord, you have examined my heart and know everything about me. You know when I sit or stand. When far away you know my every thought. You chart the path ahead of me, and tell me where to stop and rest. Every moment, you know where I am. You know what I am going to say before I even say it. You both precede and follow me, and place your hand of blessing on my head. This is too glorious, too wonderful to believe! . . . You made all the delicate, inner parts of my body, and knit them together in my mother's womb. Thank you for making me so wonderfully complex! It is amazing to think about. Your workmanship is marvelous—and how well I know it. You were there while I was being formed in utter seclusion! You saw me before I was born and scheduled each day of my life before I began to breathe. Every day was recorded in your Book! Psalm 139:1-6, 13-16 LVB*

Our Lord formed us and set our path before us. He knows where we've been and where we are going. Our Father loves us just the way we are.

He knows the exact works that we are going to do for Him. We are here to complete certain jobs for the Lord. He is the One who created us, molds us and shapes us. It's up to us not to wiggle too much in His hands while He's doing this.

> *And yet, O Lord, you are our Father. We are the clay and you are the Potter. We are all formed by your hand. Isaiah 64:8 LVB*

My Kingdom is built one soul at a time; each and every heart is important to Me. If you weren't with Me, My body would be incomplete. As I've said before, it doesn't matter how close you are to Me. It only matters that you walk My way, that you seek Me. I love you. Don't be discouraged because you are not as close to Me as others are. You will get there. Keep coming; keep walking.

I love you the same as I love the prophets of old. I can hug you just as I hug them. My love is for all, not just the strong. Just as I love the prodigal son, I love you. You are welcome in My presence any time. I adore being with you, and My desire is to bless you. Keep coming forward because I have your hand. You are doing well.

> *And a scribe came up and said to him, "Teacher, I will follow you wherever you go." Matthew 8:19 RSV*

Go where He goes, walk where He walks and stay next to God in His will.

> *As therefore ye received Christ Jesus the Lord, so walk in him, rooted and built up in him, and established in your faith, even as ye were taught, abounding in thanksgiving. Colossians 2:6-7 ASV*

Everything about you is important to Me. Everything in you and your life is extremely important to Me. I created you. I know all of your situations, and I know the outcome. The process of how you go through them is important to Me. I died for you—that is how important you are to Me! If you were not so dear to Me, I would not have given up My blood, My life, My love for you. Don't ever think you're too small to be noticed. I always have My eyes on you. My heart is always with you. It is a permanent fixture in your life, whether you know it or not. My desire is for you to know I am with you always, I love you and you can always rely on Me for anything you need. I want you to know I have given My life, My everything for you; therefore, everything I have is yours. My love is all you need; everything else just naturally comes along with it, such as grace and mercy, forgiveness and all the blessings I bestow upon you.

> *For the life of the flesh is in the blood: and I have given it to you upon the altar to make an atonement for your souls: for it is the blood that maketh an atonement for the soul. Leviticus 17:11 KJV*

Jesus died for our soul. If we weren't important to Him, He would have said no to the cross.

Everything is done for a reason. All that you have gone through is not by chance. All of your life has a purpose. Every single detail is to glorify Me. Remember all the little things, certain little positive points in your life? They were leading you to what you are doing for Me, what you are yet to do for Me. I have even turned around the negative aspects of your life. It's already done in the spiritual world. I am turning the negative around in your life, for My glory. All evil deeds show the enemy's character; therefore, I am glorified through the negative. I account for every single minute of your life. There is a purpose for each moment. I am in control; I see all. Your life is in My hands.

> *And we know that all things work together for good to them that love God, to them who are the called according to his purpose. Romans 8:28 KJV*

All that we do and have done has a purpose. All is done for God's glory. We can grow through our mistakes and failures. We can grow closer to our Father through our trials. Even the best times of our life have been ordained by God. The Lord knew every one of our joys and sorrows before the beginning of time. All of these events glorify God; they are a testimony of what our Father has done and His love toward us.

Every little thing I do for you, everything I have you do, is for a reason. Even going to the grocery store has a purpose. Somebody

there needs to see your smile, needs to talk to you or just needs to observe Jesus in your actions.

If you look back, you can see My hand in all things. You can see My protection, My guidance and My corrections all leading you back to Me. Everything has hidden benefits for you when you are with Me, in My will. Stay with Me; don't grow weary. I am still here. I will never leave you, and I will always guide you, as long as you listen. Some things you do for Me may be for a totally different purpose than you think.

> *His purpose in all of this is that they should seek after God, and perhaps feel their way toward him and find him —though he is not far from any one of us. For in him we live and move and are! As one of your own poets says it, "We are the sons of God." Acts 17:27-28 LVB*

It is our obligation to our Savior to do as He asks. When we follow His direction and guidance, we may be blessing someone around us who needed to see the love of God at that particular time.

Every righteous step is ordained by Me. I go before you, and I set your path. When you stay on My path, you reap the benefits. You receive My blessings. If you veer off, you may miss something I had planned for you. It will take longer for you to know what is in store for you. You have to get back on the path to receive what I have for you.

> *The Lord is good and glad to teach the proper path to all who go astray; he will teach the ways that are right and best to those who humbly turn to him. And when we obey him, every path he guides us on is fragrant with his lovingkindness and his truth.*
> *Psalm 25:8-10 LVB*

Jesus is our perfect example, and He wants to be our guide. He is the way to a Godly life. He is the way to eternal life, to a peaceful life. When we follow His commands, we are truly blessed. But sometimes we forget to do things His way. That's when we are not in His will; we are off His path. We merely have to remember to turn back toward His way.

> *But, Lord, my sins! How many they are. Oh, pardon them for the honor of your name. Where is the man who fears the Lord? God will teach him how to choose the best. He shall live within God's circle of blessing, and his children shall inherit the earth. Friendship with God is reserved for those who reverence him. With them alone he shares the secrets of his promises. Psalm 25:11-14 LVB*

If we are not in God's will, we can miss the blessings He had for us. Thankfully, we can easily get back on track by just asking for forgiveness. We can receive His showers of blessings again. We can live in the promises He has for us. God has wonderful plans for us when we are walking with Him hand-in-hand.

Can I Use You For A Minute? — God

When you obey and do My will, I can use you for My glory. Stay on track, and don't waver. You can go further and further with Me when you stay with Me. Even when you do go off track a little bit, I still love you. Just keep looking My way. I will fill you. The more you give up, the more I can fill you with My goodness. I alone want to live in your temple. Empty yourself, and let My love overtake you. You will shine for Me. Others will see Me in you; just keep going forth in My ways.

> *So, get your minds ready. Be alert. Put your hope completely upon the gracious love that you will receive when Jesus Christ appears. Like children who always obey, don't be controlled by the evil desires you used to have when you didn't know any better. Instead, in all your life be holy, as God is holy. He called you. This is written: "You must be holy because I am holy!" 1 Peter 1:13-16 SIM*

We are called to be holy like God so others can see His love. We are His vessel and should be available for Him at all times.

> *This is what the Lord commanded us to do: "I have made you a light for other nations, so that you may show the way of salvation to people all over the world." Acts 13:47 SIM*

When we say no to ourselves and yes to the Lord, we are letting God fill us with His light and His love. This love is what is shown to the world. Obeying His word brings His blessings into our lives. Being God's temple—what else could we want to be used for?

All My children are different, but I love them all the same amount. There is not one that I do not love. I hurt for My children, just as you hurt for the ones you love, only more so. I created them, yet they don't look My way. I have brought them into this world; I breathed life into them, yet they can't see Me or acknowledge Me. They don't pay attention to Me. I speak, yet they do not hear. I am grateful for those who hear. I am proud to be their Father. I will use them. I am using them to help others see and hear. I use them to bring others home to Me. Obedience is wonderful; it helps get My work done for Me. It brings My children closer to Me. There isn't much time left, though. I am gathering all My children soon, so obey, that all My loved ones can enter in.

> *And in thy seed shall all the nations of the earth be blessed; because thou hast obeyed my voice. Genesis 22:18 KJV*

Listen and obey. It benefits everyone.

I desire that others see Me through you. You are My temple. I want people to know I am alive in you; therefore, My blessings are upon you so others can see Me in you. I am the answer to all their problems. You are My temple to which they can run. I am using you for My purpose. I created you. I breathed My breath into you; I gave you life. I gave you My Son. Your life is through My Son because He died for you. I pour My love upon you that it will flow through you to others. You are My willing vessel. I am using you for My purpose, to deliver My love to others. I love you more than you understand.

Do you not know that your body is a temple of the Holy Spirit within you, which you have from God? You are not your own; you were bought with a price. So glorify God in your body.
1 Corinthians 6:19-20 RSV

Let the Lord use you for His glory.
He gave you life, why not live for Him?

If ye be willing and obedient, ye shall eat the good of the land:
Isaiah 1:19 KJV

Your obedience pleases Me. My blessings can flow through you and to you. I can use you when you obey. I love to bless you. I pour My blessings upon you when you obey.

AND IF you obey the voice of the Lord your God, being careful to do all his commandments which I command you this day, the Lord your God will set you high above all the nations of the earth. And all these blessings shall come upon you and overtake you, if you obey the voice of the Lord your God. Blessed shall you be in the city, and blessed shall you be in the field. Blessed shall be the fruit of your body, and the fruit of your ground, and the fruit of your beasts, the increase of your cattle, and the young of your flock. Blessed shall be your basket and your kneading-trough. Blessed shall you be when you come in, and blessed shall you be when you go out.

The Lord will cause your enemies who rise against you to be defeated before you; they shall come out against you one way, and flee before you seven ways. The Lord will command the blessing upon you in your barns, and in all that you undertake; and he will bless you in the land which the Lord your God gives you.

> *The Lord will establish you as a people holy to himself, as he has sworn to you, if you keep the commandments of the Lord your God, and walk in his ways. And all the peoples of the earth shall see that you are called by the name of the Lord; and they shall be afraid of you. And the Lord will make you abound in prosperity, in the fruit of your body, and in the fruit of your cattle, and in the fruit of your ground, within the land which the Lord swore to your fathers to give you. The Lord will open to you his good treasury the heavens, to give the rain of your land in its season and to bless all the work of your hands; and you shall lend to many nations, but you shall not borrow. And the Lord will make you the head, and not the tail; and you shall tend upward only, and not downward; if you obey the commandments of the Lord your God, which I command you this day, being careful to do them, and if you do not turn aside from any of the words which I command you this day, to the right hand or to the left, to go after other gods to serve them. Deuteronomy 28:1-14 RSV*

We couldn't ask for much more than that! All we have to do is say, "Yes, Lord." We don't know what kind of blessings we miss out on by not saying yes. We have no idea what He had planned for us, had we walked down the right path. As long as we stay in His will, we can receive what He has for us. He pours His blessings on us when we are with Him.

> *Behold, I set before you this day a blessing and a curse; A blessing, if ye obey the commandments of the Lord your God, which I command you this day: And a curse, if ye will not obey the commandments of the Lord your God, but turn aside out of the way which I command you this day, to go after other Gods, which ye have not known. Deuteronomy 11:26-28 KJV*

Sometimes when you expect the same things to happen over and over, they become mundane to you. Please don't let My presence become just an ordinary thing that you expect, for it

will become dull to you. I like to be exciting in your life. I am new each day; I bring you newness each day. When I ask you to look at something or to do something, I need it done, or I want to bless you for obeying. If you wait too long, you could miss the blessing. Learn to do as I ask, when I ask. I don't want you missing out on anything I have to give you. You do not know what I have in store for you at the time of obedience. I teach you new lessons each day, to give you wisdom and blessings. The blessings I give are not the same ones repeated over and over. They are not boring. My blessings are exciting.

> *If they obey and serve him, they shall spend their days in prosperity, and their years in pleasures. Job 36:11 KJV*

Simple obedience brings us so much more of God's blessings than we can ever know. When we say, "Yes, Lord," His goodness flows through us and onto others. God wishes to give us the goodness that He has already planned for us. It is waiting for us. We receive the awesome prosperity and pleasures He has for us by simply obeying His voice. None of this is ever boring.

You Are My Child — God

You are My child. You are My temple. I have deposited and will continue to deposit My love into you. My love comes from Heaven above. I am always reigning (and raining) on and in you.

> *See how very much our heavenly Father loves us, for he allows us to be called his children —think of it —and we really are! But since most people don't know God, naturally they don't understand that we are his children. 1 John 3:1 LVB*

Many of us don't realize we really are God's children. He poured out His blood for us; therefore, accepting this, we have His bloodline. We are the Lord's children, made in His image. We are His temple. We belong to the Lord Himself. He pours His love and goodness into us continually. When we accept Jesus in our heart, His Spirit lives within us.

> *Do you not know that you are God's temple and that God's Spirit dwells in you? 1 Corinthians 3:16 RSV*

My children are My joy. I look forward to hearing "Good morning" from them. Their conversations bring Me joy, like kisses to the heart. My children are like sparkling dew drops in the sunshine. They are gems in My eyes. Some are purer and clearer than others, but I am the One polishing them. If they

stay in My presence, I can clean and shine them. I can work on them, with them, in them.

If they run from Me, it will be harder on them. I won't clean them if they don't want to be cleansed. They run into the darkness, yet there is no reason to run. I am a loving God. The enemy tells them differently. He tells them lies so they run. Disobedience requires punishment, but I am a kind, loving, gentle God. I am still in them. My word is in their heart from the beginning. Pray the little sparkle left in them comes shining through and lights their way back. My children are My joy.

> *On that day the Lord their God will save them for they are the flock of his people; for like the jewels of a crown they shall shine on his land.*
> *Zechariah 9:16 RSV*

Our Father likes to see us clean and clear. He wants us to shine for others to see His glory. He is the One cleansing us. He knows exactly where our dirty spots are. When we obey His Holy Spirit and live in truth, we can shine for the Lord. His unlimited grace takes our sins away and replaces them with His holy righteousness. He wants all of His children to shine.

> *Now Joshua was standing before the angel, clothed with filthy garments. And the angel said to those who were standing before him, "Remove the filthy garments from him." And to him he said, "Behold, I have taken your iniquity away from you, and I will clothe you with rich apparel." And I said, "Let them put a clean turban on his head." So they put a clean turban on his head and clothed him with garments; and the angel of the Lord was standing by. Zechariah 3:3-5 RSV*

You are beautiful to your Heavenly Father, and you bring joy to Him when you walk in His righteousness.

> *No greater joy can I have than this, to hear that my children follow the truth. 3 John 1:4 RSV*

Just as you do not like your child to play in mud and filth, I do not like to see My children covered in sin. My children are beautiful to Me. I created them.

> *On that day there shall be a fountain opened for the house of David and the inhabitants of Jerusalem to cleanse them from sin and uncleanness. Zechariah 13:1 RSV*

Jesus is that fountain that cleanses. He's all we need. Our Lord and Savior purges all unrighteousness from us, making us clean and pure. Our Lord created us in His image, holy and beautiful. Jesus washes all our sins away when we ask forgiveness.

I am a gentle God. I am a loving God. I prefer to be gentle. I am slow to anger. If I have to be stern, I can be. It is My preference to be gentle. Some of My children need to be disciplined sternly, though My children prefer My loving kindness. I want you, My child, to see My ways. I am brilliant and bright. I want you to see Me clearly, to walk on My path without stumbling or trying to guess which way to go. Just open your heart and listen. I am always near you. I surround you. Distractions come into your life, but just keep focused on Me. If you're not sure, just ask Me.

The Lord is our Father and our guide. Staying focused on our Father and His love is the most important thing we can do. Not only do we benefit from it by staying in His will, but those who are around us can know His love, also. If we fail, we only have to turn back to Him.

> *RETURN, O Israel, to the Lord your God, for you have stumbled because of your iniquity. Take with you words and return to the Lord; say to him, "Take away all iniquity; accept that which is good and we will render the fruit of our lips." Hosea 14:1-2 RSV*

Our Father gladly picks us up and takes us back into His loving arms when we ask forgiveness for our wrongs.

> *With weeping they shall come, and with consolations I will lead them back, I will make them walk by brooks of water, in a straight path in which they shall not stumble; Jeremiah 31:9 RSV*

My children are important to Me. They are My heart. Your children are My children. I love them no matter what they do, no matter where they have been. I always welcome them home. This was the purpose of My Son's death on the cross—to bring My children back from sin. He took care of the cost. My children are beckoned to come home. I dust them off; I clean them up. They will be righteous, and I will make them pure and holy.

Your children are My children. Keep praising Me that they have come home. It is already written; therefore, they will turn around and be here soon. Like the prodigal son that turned back to his father whom he knew loved him before, so your children will turn back to Me.

> *Then Jesus said, "A man had two sons. The younger son said to his father, 'Father, give me my part of all our holdings!' So, the father divided the property with his two sons. Not long afterward, the younger son gathered up all that he had and left. He traveled far away to another country. There the son wasted his money like a fool; he spent everything he had. Then the land became very dry, and it did not rain.*

> *There was not enough food to eat anywhere in that country. He began to starve. So, he went and got a job with one of the important men of that country. The man sent him into the fields to feed pigs. The boy was so hungry, that he wanted to stuff himself with the food which the pigs were eating. No one was giving him anything. Finally, the boy realized that he had been very foolish. He thought, All of my father's servants have plenty of food, yet here I am about to die, because I have nothing to eat. I will get up and go to my father. I will say to him: 'Father, I sinned against God and in front of you. I'm not worthy to be called your son anymore. Treat me as one of your paid servants.' So, the son got up and went to his father. The son said, 'Father, I sinned against God and in front of you. I'm not worthy to be called your son anymore.' But the father said to his servants, 'Hurry! Bring the best robe and dress him. Put a ring on his finger and shoes on his feet, too. Bring our fattened calf. We will kill it and have plenty to eat. Then we can have a party! My son was dead, but now he is alive again . . . he was lost, but now he is found!' So, they began to celebrate." Luke 15:11-24 SIM*

Our Father loves us no matter what condition we are in. There is no sin too big for Him to forgive because our God is bigger. All He wants is to hear our heart cry out in forgiveness. Our Father has promised us that the children He has blessed us with will be saved, also.

> *And they said, "Believe in the Lord Jesus, and you will be saved, you and your household." Acts 16:31 RSV*

Tell Them I Love Them, Too — God

You have entered into My presence. You love to be in My presence, and I love to be with you, but just think of those who have not known My presence. There are those who have never known Me, what I have for them: My grace, My mercy, My love and forgiveness. Invite them into My house. Speak to them of Me; show them My Son, Jesus, so they, too, can enter into My presence, so they can enter into My gates. My house is big; I have enough love for everyone. I share My love; My love covers all. Invite them into My house.

> *And the lord said unto the servant, Go out into the highways and hedges, and compel them to come in, that my house may be filled.*
> *Luke 14:23 KJV*

The Lord gave us a command. We are to tell everyone else about His love. His house is big, and He wants it filled with His children. Our Father is family oriented. He yearns for all His children to be safe at home with Him. There are many people who don't know how much their Creator loves them, and it is our job to tell them. We can give them joy by giving them the word of God.

It's time to tell them. Time to tell them to turn around. Ask them to come home. Tell them I love them. I will reveal who is ready to you. I will lead you to the ones who will listen, because I have prepared their hearts.

I have been drawing them. Hear Me when I tell you it's time. I have not given you a spirit of fear or rejection. That is from the adversary. When I tell you it's time, just do it. When I tell you it's time, speak to them. Display My love, they will be looking for it. Tell them it's time they turn My way. You have the victory over the enemy's lies about them. He has lost. You will do well to help Me in My work.

> *Brethren, my heart's desire and my supplication to God is for them, that they may be saved. Romans 10:1 ASV*

When you ask, you receive. If you don't ask, you might never receive. This is why I tell you to pray. Praying is asking. This is why I tell you to pray for the lost, that I bring them in, that I will draw their hearts. I will answer your prayers so that you can receive. I always say yes to requests of salvation, for they are My children. It is in My heart to see them safe in My bosom. Keep praying; keep asking. I hear your requests, and I will grant them.

> *And the prayer of faith shall save the sick, and the Lord shall raise him up; and if he have committed sins, they shall be forgiven him. James 5:15 KJV*

If My people would pray and seek My face, I will show them the way to righteousness. They will see the Light. I have won the battle. You are on the right track; keep going. Keep praying, keep seeking that others may see the way and walk the right path. I am going across the land. Revival is coming. I love your praises, I want more people praising and praying. Pray that they come in. Pray they come into the Kingdom.

> *If my people, which are called by my name, shall humble themselves, and pray, and seek my face, and turn from their wicked ways; then will I hear from heaven, and will forgive their sin, and will heal their land. 2 Chronicles 7:14 KJV*

When God's people pray and seek Him, look for His ways, walk with Him and no longer walk in their own ways, He hears their prayers. He heals hearts, and He fixes problems. God forgives our sins when we ask with a humble heart. All we have to do is stay in His will and look for Him in every situation. He is the answer for the believer and the unbeliever. Your desire should be as the Father's—to have every soul saved from Hell.

They don't know what they're missing. Invite them in so they can see what My Spirit can do for them. Invite them into My house. Invite them into your heart. The only thing that matters is My love. I want to give it away. I want to give it to My people. Tell them to come. I desire their worship. I want to love on My children. I desire their presence. I want them to come home just as you desire your children to be close to you. They are in My heart. I will draw them; you invite them. My coming is soon, and there is not much time. Keep spreading My word. I love you, My child. I love them as much as I love you. I want them to be true worshippers deep in their hearts.

> *Go ye therefore into the highways, and as many as ye shall find, bid to the marriage. So those servants went out into the highways, and gathered together all as many as they found, both bad and good: and the wedding was furnished with guests. Matthew 22:9-10 KJV*

Our Father invites everyone into His Kingdom. God loves His family, all His children. The children who know Jesus Christ are the ones sent out with an invitation for the ones yet to come. All His children are welcome to celebrate the Lord. Soon, we will have one great big family reunion.

> *How blessed those whom you choose and invite to dwell in your courts. We shall be filled with the good things of your house, of your holy temple. Psalm 65:4 NJB*

We become filled with His goodness when we accept the invitation handed to us—an invitation to come into God's house and live forever. Our hearts are filled with joy and praises toward Him. Our Father desires that we worship Him. We are encouraged to invite the lost to become true worshippers of the Almighty God with us.

I put people in your path so you can pray for them each time you remember them. People from your childhood, people from your neighborhood, people from your classroom and work place are all important to Me. They were all brought into your life for a reason; nothing is by accident. Some were a blessing to you; others were not. Regardless of what they did to or for you, pray for them. Some have already turned to Me, but still pray My blessing upon them and their family. I want to bless them even more. You do not know exactly what is going on in their lives; I do. Pray for them. Everyone can use prayer; everyone can use My blessings. I will grant your requests in My will. You ask and believe; therefore, you receive, even for others. Pray they accept the blessings—not one blessing, but all My blessings, all My gifts.

> *First of all, I beg you to pray for all people. Ask for things. Speak for them. Be thankful to God for them. Pray for kings and all those who have authority, so that we may lead peaceful, quiet lives. We want to be godly and serious. This is good and acceptable before God, our Savior. God wants all men to be saved and to begin understanding the truth.*
> *1 Timothy 2:1-4 SIM*

Shine This Light So They Can See — God

❦

I am sending you into the darkness, but worry not. I will be with you. I am your Light, and I have given you the Light. I will not leave you. I will be holding your hand. You have work to do for Me.

> I am the Lord, I have called you in righteousness, I have taken you by the hand and kept you; I have given you as a covenant to the people, a light to the nations, to open the eyes that are blind, to bring out the prisoners from the dungeon, from the prison those who sit in darkness. Isaiah 42:6-7 RSV

Those of us who know the Lord are handpicked to go to the ones who have not received Him yet. We are to show them the way. God sends the unknowing our way so we can enlighten them to His mercy. We are sent to the ones who are still in the darkness to tell them about the Lord's love. Our Father is always with us, holding our hand, encouraging us to help bring others Light.

> Nevertheless I am continually with thee: thou hast holden me by my right hand. Psalm 73:23 KJV

I want My River to flow; My River will flow through you. My glory will shine on you. My Light will shine through you.

> *He that believeth on me, as the scripture hath said, out of his belly shall flow rivers of living water. John 7:38 KJV*

God's river of love never stops flowing. He is love. His being is love. He always wants His glory and joy to flow over and surround everyone. Our Father wants to use His children to let His river flow. This is how His glory is seen. When you yield to the Lord and let Him use you, others can see His Light, His righteousness and goodness. People will be able to see His love through you as you get to know Him more. Others will see the joy that only comes from having Jesus within. God's river of life flows through you to others.

My Light can go to the deepest, darkest places. Just as light directs a reflection, so My Light directs you, My reflection, My image. Hear Me; go where I tell you to go.

> *Hearken diligently to the trembling of his voice, Yea, the sound from his mouth goeth forth. Under the whole heavens he directeth it, And its light [is] over the skirts of the earth. Job 37:2-3 YGB*

The King James Version of the Bible reads "lightning" instead of "light." Light comes from the Romanized word "owr," which means illumination—in every sense, including lightning and happiness, to set on fire, to shine, to make luminous, glorious and kindle. We are God's light when we have Jesus in us. He will use us to bring happiness to the earth, to give out His word. We can set the earth on fire with His love. God will use us to illuminate the dark places in the world. We are His reflection.

> *But we Christians have no veil over our faces; we can be mirrors that brightly reflect the glory of the Lord. And as the Spirit of the Lord works within us, we become more and more like him.*
> *2 Corinthians 3:18 LVB*

We behold His glory; we can do as He does. We are the image of God's love, power and strength. We are to reflect who the Lord is and what He does.

My Light is shining through. My Light is coming forth through the darkness. It will not be long. Only My Light can show the way. Man's light can only shine so far. His light has boundaries. With it, you cannot see the whole picture; you can only see so far. It is artificial. My Light is real and is forever. There are no boundaries in My Light. When My Light shines through, it comes fast and reveals all. Darkness flees; it cannot overtake the Light. My beauty shines through in the Light. My Light is Jesus. Jesus is coming soon. He is coming quickly. He is ready to go forth. My Word is always ready to go forth. Jesus is the Way.

When you are in darkness, just reach up and call out, and I will hear you. As the clouds blot out the light, the Son is still above the clouds. Reach through the darkness; reach through the cloudiness if you don't understand; keep reaching through the circumstances that surround you. My Son is above all. He hears and sees all. His Light reveals all.

> *The people who walked in darkness have seen a great light; those who dwelt in a land of deep darkness, on them has light shined.*
> *Isaiah 9:2 RSV*

If we could just remember to look for the Lord first in every situation. We have to reach into that thick darkness where God is, away from what we know, and into His wisdom. He is the true Light, the One that shines through. Our Lord reveals which path to take. His ways are laid forth before us to see. When we are walking in darkness, all we have to do is look to God for the light. Our God changes our hearts, changes our lives when we look to Him.

> *For God, who commanded the light to shine out of darkness, hath shined in our hearts, to give the light of the knowledge of the glory of God in the face of Jesus Christ. 2 Corinthians 4:6 KJV*

There are enough non-Christians out there without the Christians not believing My full word. I want My children to trust Me and live for Me completely. I want all to believe in Me. Miracles are for those who don't believe in Jesus, so they can see Me and know My ways. All who believe are to trust with their whole heart, not just part. Look to Me and Me only. Do not look off to the side because you will not see the truth. There is only one way to look, only one way to see the light. It gets diffused when looking elsewhere. Believe in Me; I am the Light.

"To diffuse" means "to spread out or scatter, less concentrated, to make less brilliant." The enemy tries to diffuse God's word. God's word is total truth. His word is the only truth. Just because we don't believe or know God's word, does not make it any less true or good.

> *For what if some did not believe? Shall their unbelief make the faith of God without effect? God forbid: yea, let God be true, but every man a liar; as it is written, That thou mightest be justified in thy sayings, and mightest overcome when thou art judged. Romans 3:3-4 KJV*

Even as believers of Jesus Christ, we have to keep accepting and receiving <u>every</u> word our Lord has for us and believe the WHOLE Bible. God gives us new wisdom, knowledge, comfort and peace daily when we seek Him and look His way.

> *Jesus cried and said, he that believeth on me, believeth not on me, but on him that sent me. And he that seeth me seeth him that sent me. I am come a light into the world, that whosoever believeth on me should not abide in darkness. John 12:44-46 KJV*

*There is no darkness in our life
when we are in God's light.*

**Without the understanding of My love you will be cold and
unloving. My mercy goes deep for you. Lost souls cannot find
their way. You must go into the darkness. You are the light. You
must go into the darkness to be able to reach and understand.
You must understand My mercy. Pray and seek My love, My
understanding and My mercy.**

**I am a burning fire. Pray and seek so that you will be equipped.
Seek Me. I am counting on you. I will give you those things
(equipment) because I want you to have all that is needed. Seek
Me, morning, noon and night.**

> *As the people stood in the distance, Moses entered into the deep
> darkness where God was. And the Lord told Moses to be his
> spokesman to the people of Israel. You are witnesses to the fact that I
> have made known my will to you from heaven. Exodus 20:21-22 LVB*

To those who do not know the Lord intimately, God is in the thick
darkness. Moses went into the thick darkness where God was for
the benefit of the people who didn't understand the things of the
Lord. Moses went into the unknown places of God. God is so holy
and so divine; His love is so vast that we can be literally in the dark
about how perfect and awesome He is. We can be in the dark about
His greatness and truth. His love is considered deep and dark to
those who don't know. God is the perfect light. This light can shine
on all who will seek and choose to understand. As children of God,
we can choose to go into the unknown of God and be enlightened.
Ignorance and unbelief can turn to faith and understanding.

**The more you seek Me, the more others will want what I give
you; others will want to come home. More souls will turn to Me.**

Others will want My love; they will want My Spirit. They will want My peace. Others will seek after Me.

If people do not see Me anywhere, how will they know what they want? How will they know what goodness and love look like?

They can only have the world to look forward to if that is all they see. Keep walking with Me; others will want to follow.

> *As you know, God has appointed me as a special messenger to you Gentiles. I lay great stress on this and remind the Jews about it as often as I can, so that if possible I can make them want what you Gentiles have and in that way save some of them. And how wonderful it will be when they become Christians! When God turned away from them it meant that he turned to the rest of the world to offer his salvation; and now it is even more wonderful when the Jews come to Christ. It will be like dead people coming back to life.*
> *Romans 11:13 LVB*

My glory is here. My joy is here. Receive it. You are home when you are in My presence. You have My Spirit; you are My child, and you have always been My child. I picked you a long time ago. Receive My blessings. Play in My words; play in My water. Jump in because I am here. When others see you playing, they will want to join you. My children will want to play along with you; they will want to be in My presence. I am the victor, and I am the conqueror. Others will come, so keep praying. They are on their way. Keep seeking. You have broken down barriers. They (loved ones) are coming. I am the victor.

Jesus is the living water. Our Creator designed us to live in His love long ago. He likes to see us enjoy ourselves. Others around us will see our joy and peace. They will want what we have. They will seek it, and the Lord is more than willing to give His love to them.

When the poor and needy seek water, and there is none, and their tongue is parched with thirst, I the Lord will answer them, I the God of Israel will not forsake them. I will open rivers on the bare heights, and fountains in the midst of the valleys; I will make the wilderness a pool of water, and the dry land springs of water. Isaiah 41:17-18 RSV

Don't Be A Fool—God

All My children have the opportunity to see Me. Some choose not to; some just don't know. They choose to look the other way. They don't want to see the light. It's too bright, and it reveals all sin. My nature is peaceful; it is calm; it is togetherness; it is beautiful. My nature is not confusion. My nature is all around and with you all the time. It is everywhere. The more you study and seek My face, the more you will find of Me. I will reveal My nature to you. I will also reveal more of the enemy's nature. You'll be able to see his little tricks and his little tracks. You'll know what to pray against. You'll see how he works. He sneaks around, trying to hide from the light. He doesn't want anybody to see his true nature, so he tries to imitate the light. The enemy is afraid of the true light.

> *This is the verdict: Light has come into the world, but people loved darkness more than they loved light because the things which they were doing were evil. Everyone who does evil hates the light. He does not come toward the light. He doesn't want his evil deeds to be exposed. But the person who is living the truth comes toward the light. He wants his actions to become clear, because he did them for God.*
> *John 3:19-21 SIM*

The enemy is insecure and wants to pass that insecurity on to others by appealing to their flesh. Selfishness is his motivation. He tells people to please their selves, their flesh, their own wants and desires. Pride and selfishness are from the devil. Out of these come the love of money, drugs, lustfulness, adultery, murder, even complaining. I abhor these things; they are not of Me.

> *Know this: There will be hard times during the last days. People will be selfish, greedy, boastful, proud, blasphemers, disobeying their parents, unthankful, unholy, without natural love, unforgiving, gossips, violent, mean, hating good, traitors, wild, and conceited. They will love pleasures more than they love God. 2 Timothy 3:1-4 SIM*

Confusion comes from the enemy, also. He doesn't want My people to see the way; he is selfish and wants them to stay in the dark with him. He doesn't want them to know Me. The adversary keeps a dark veil over their eyes so they don't see.

> *And even if our gospel is veiled, it is veiled only to those who are perishing. In their case the god of this world has blinded the minds of the unbelievers, to keep them from seeing the light of the gospel of the glory of Christ, who is the likeness of God. 2 Corinthians 4:3-4 RSV*

I will remove the veil from those who seek Me. If they would just call for Me, I will reach out to them. I will reveal Myself to them, and I will reveal My nature to them. My children can have all that I have for them, all that I have in store for them. Keep praying that they look My way; I am not forceful. I want them to ask Me, look for Me, seek Me. They need to turn their heads, turn their eyes My way.

> *Yes, to this day whenever Moses is read a veil lies over their minds; but when a man turns to the Lord the veil is removed. Now the Lord is the Spirit, and where the Spirit of the Lord is, there is freedom. And we all, with unveiled face, beholding the glory of the Lord, are being changed into his likeness from one degree of glory to another; for this comes from the Lord who is the Spirit. 2 Corinthians 3:15-18 RSV*

Our Father wants everyone to see His light so we can walk in His blessings. He desires that we seek after Him so we can be knowledgeable and wise in His ways, then we can distinguish the ways of the enemy. We are to know our adversary so we don't fall into his evil traps. It's our job as Christians to pray for the ones who have their eyes elsewhere so they, too, can see the light and live in God's glory completely.

> *Evil men understand not judgment: but they that seek the Lord understand all things. Proverbs 28:5 KJV*

Fools like to talk about themselves and stir up chaos. They like attention. They are within themselves. They live for themselves. Fools are greedy. The more attention they get, the more they like it. They are satisfied with their self-attention. They wallow in it. Do not be near fools; do not give them what they want. They will draw you in. Don't fall into their trap. It is called self-pity. Whether they are happy and content at the time or lonely and miserable, they like to be within themselves and let other people see it.

Do not focus on them, but pray for them. A fool likes to run his mouth; he likes to stir up trouble. He is content in confusion. If there is nobody looking his way, he will find a reason—any reason—to get the attention of others. This is why he cannot keep his money. It is flaunted so people will look. It is a way of getting attention. A fool and his money are soon parted, no matter how much he has. A fool brings his family misery and bitterness. The enemy is running rampant and trying to keep people foolish.

Pray for them; I will draw them. They will hear. Time is getting nearer, and I am coming very soon. Pray harder for them. Pray harder for the lost ones; listen to My voice; listen for Me.

> *The way of a fool is right in his own eyes: but he that hearkeneth unto counsel is wise. Proverbs 12:15 KJV*

Proverbs 1, 10, 12, 13, 14, 15, 17 and 26 show differences between the foolish and the wise. Ecclesiastes also teaches about how the foolish and the wise live. Fools can ask for forgiveness, turn from their ways and receive wisdom. Pray for them.

> *But I say unto you, Love your enemies, bless them that curse you, do good to them that hate you, and pray for them which despitefully use you, and persecute you; That ye may be the children of your Father which is in heaven: for he maketh his sun to rise on the evil and on the good, and sendeth rain on the just and on the unjust. Matthew 5:44-45 KJV*

I Have The Perfect Plan For You — God

I know the plans I have for you, plans to prosper you, plans to give you hope.

> *For I know the plans I have for you, says the Lord. They are plans for good and not for evil, to give you a future and a hope.*
> *Jeremiah 29:11 LVB*

God has awesome blessings in store for us. He has beautiful plans for our lives with Him. If we would only seek Him, listen for His voice and find out what they are—

May mercy, peace and love be multiplied to you.

> *Mercy unto you, and peace, and love, be multiplied. Jude 1:2 KJV*

The Lord is mercy. He knows we need mercy, and He offers it to us without boundaries. Mercy and goodness follow us everywhere (Psalm 23:6). God has immeasurable compassion for us. He wants us to have a wonderful life. He desires us to live in peace with ourselves and with others. God enjoys seeing us content. He wants us to live in love; He wants it multiplied to us, for us to live in love abundantly. We receive these blessings and our eyes are opened to these benefits when we come closer to the Lord; when we long for His presence; when we know His love.

Lynn Marie White

> *And the very God of peace sanctify you wholly; and I pray God your whole spirit and soul and body be preserved blameless unto the coming of our Lord Jesus Christ. 1 Thessalonians 5:23 KJV*